Shitten Shepherds & Clene Sheep

*The title of this book was derived from Geofrey Chauser's *The Canterbury Tales*

Shitten Shepherds & Clene Sheep

Unmasking the True Causes
of the Scandals in the
Catholic Church

JOSEPH COPPERSON

*The title of this book was derived from Geofrey Chauser's *The Canterbury Tales*

Charleston, SC
www.PalmettoPublishing.com

Shitten Shepherds and Clene Sheep
Copyright © 2023 by Joseph Copperson

All rights reserved
No portion of this book may be reproduced, stored in a retrieval system, or transmitted in any form by any means—electronic, mechanical, photocopy, recording, or other—except for brief quotations in printed reviews, without prior permission of the author.

First Edition

Hardcover ISBN: 979-8-8229-1742-2
Paperback ISBN: 979-8-8229-1743-9
eBook ISBN: 979-8-8229-1744-6

The title is drawn from The Canterbury Tales by Geoffrey Chaucer. Written between 1387 and his death in 1400, it is not only Chaucer's best known work but the most famous literary work in Middle English. It is one of the finest works of English literature. Chaucer is hailed to this day as the first great English poet.*

To exist is to change
To change is to mature
To mature is to go on creating oneself endlessly
Herni Bergson

Dedication

To my daughter in-law the most insightful guide

Table of Contents

Introduction i
Prologue ii

Chapter 1: Newly ordained priest. Home in America. A new life begins. 1
Chapter 2: The Beginning. My first assignment as the summer priest. 7
Chapter 3: First encounter with the entrenched clerical culture. 11
Chapter 4: Difficulties with the clerical culture intensifies. 19
Chapter 5: The joy of helping others learns that God has created all of us in His Own *image*. 29
Chapter 6: More corruption within the clerical culture revealed. 37
Chapter 7: The joys and challenges of the learning process. 43
Chapter 8: The decade of the 1960's continued. 51
Chapter 9: My last years at St. Marc's. The decade of the 60's closes. 61
Chapter 10: Concluding perspectives in the present time. 73

Epilogue 79
Appendix I 87
   (The writings of the authors whose words are cited in the text.)
Appendix II 89
   (A select bibliography of writers and their works that have inspired the author's thinking)

Introduction

As a newly ordained American parish priest I hit the cultural upheaval of thle1960's head on. During four years of intense theological education in Europe. I was totally absorbed in the proposed revolutionary renewal that was Vatican II. This memoir contains the stories that influenced my life. They are stories of my interaction with a significant number of Catholic priests. Some of these priests lived a life of hypocrisy, deceit, greed and arrogance. I will argue that the corrupt clerical culture contains the **true causes** of violent crimes against innocent children, women, young men, sexuality and human dignity itself. This book has been more than fifty years in development. The stories are true. They seek to shine a spotlight on scandals now threatening the faith of so many Catholics in the United States and in many nations throughout the world. It will offer actions needed to address the great Scandals in the Catholic Church.

These proposed actions are unquestionably revolutionary.

This book is certainly appropriate for our time.

SCANDALS IN THE CATHOLIC CHURCH
A MEMOIR
I AM A WITNESS

Perhaps Geoffrey Chaucer, the first great poet in the English language, said it colorfully and best when he wrote in the 14th century that there is something horribly wrong in the Catholic Church when there are "shitten shepherds and clean sheep".

> And shame it is, if a preest take keep, for if a preest be foul, on whom we truste
> No wonder is a lewed man to ruste; a shitten shepherde and a clene sheep.
> Wel oghte a preest ensample for to yive, by his cleanness, how that his sheep sholde lyve.*
>
> Geoffrey Chaucer – The Canterbury Tales,
> General Prologue, II, 503-8.

(I will interject throughout this book, references to Chaucer's words in this story. They will be brief comments written in Old English Text. Usually there will be a rewrite in contemporary English in italics as is here.)

For if a priest be sinful in whom we trust no wonder is a sinful man to fail, and shame it is, if a priest betray his promises, he is then a corrupt hypocritical shepherd among his innocent sheep. For a priest ought to give a clear example by his holiness of life how his people should live.

Prologue

This book contains the stories that so influenced my life as a young newly appointed American parish priest and college professor in the cultural upheaval decade of the 1960's. Stories really matter. They matter enormously. Stories are not just a big thing. They are often the most important thing. Although limited in a specific time in history, the 1960's, these stories do involve my encounters with a significant number of corrupt American Catholic priests. These men betrayed their original commitment to serve as shepherds of the people of the Roman Catholic Church community in the United States. These priests became, in Chaucer's colorful words, ***shitten shepherds among the clene sheep***. However, by no means are these stories of hypocritical and arrogant men the stories of all or even most American Catholic priests in the 1960's. Nor do they include the stories of many priests both in Europe and America who I admired and whose friendship I cherish to this day. Though it may happen, they are not stories told to shock or offend. There are countless people who admire the many humble and compassionate priests both living and deceased they encountered. These priests dedicated themselves as good shepherds in the service of their people. But these are the stories of a large number of irresponsible priests. They knowingly chose an arrogant, deceitful and corrupt way of thinking and behaving. This choice engaged them in a life of hypocrisy, deceit and greed. Clearly the **world view** of many founding fathers of the United States was often formed by racist beliefs. So too a significant number of American Catholic priests' minds were formed by archaic corrupt ways of thinking. Scripture relates that the Lord Jesus warned his disciples to ***Beware the Leaven of the Pharisees***, an evil hypocrisy practiced by many leaders of Judaism in the early days of Christianity. This ***Leaven of the Pharisees*** was often warned against by early Christian leaders. It seems to be completely invisible to many Catholic priests and even some bishops noted here. Liked the Pharisee caste of the biblical era, these men believed **only** *they* had total command of the truth. They believed their pronouncements were **the very will of God**. For far too many the warning: **Beware the Leaven of the Pharisees** fell on deaf ears. It seems that for far too many this *leaven* of superiority, exclusivity and entitlement remains alive and well even into the 21st century.

In 1962, at the close of the first session of the Preparatory Leadership Council of the Roman Catholic Church being held in Vatican City the Austrian bishop delegation composed a joint letter to Pope John XXIII, concerning the calling of this world wide gathering of Catholic Leaders, known as an Ecumenical Council. In the letter they predicted that the unprecedented changes for renewal promoted by the mildly revolutionary proposals of this Council would not succeed. They wrote that the majority of reforms would be rejected by many of the clergy caste. This rejection would be made not only by priests but even members of the senior leadership now assembled in Rome. They wrote that perhaps there would be many bishops, cardinals and even possibly a future pope himself who would seek to overturn the proposals of this Council forever to be known as The Second Vatican Council or **Vatican II.** Their warning was most prescient.

> *(Like the chorus in the classical Greek dramas, I will often offer a perspective based upon knowledge possessed in the present. These comments as the following one demonstrates will appear in italics encased in parentheses.*
>
> *It was if the Austrian Bishops had seen the future. In this future a large numbers of Catholic priests, bishops and even cardinals would be incapable of comprehending, let alone prepared to accept the proposals of Vatican II. Its open and inclusive vision of a renewed Roman Catholic society would*

Prologue

soon be undermined then put aside after the soon to take place death of Pope John XXIII. His three immediate successors saw to that. They were Paul VI, John Paul II and Benedict XVI.)

Today in these early years of the 21st century a flood tide of scandals has emerged overwhelming the Roman Catholic Community throughout the world. Geoffrey Chaucer's words echo through the centuries with greater force than ever: *(in contemporary English- If a priest be corrupt in whom we have trusted, it is no wonder that a poor layman lose his faith.)*

Without any doubt, the horrible crimes against children by priests and bishops in the United States and throughout the world need to be thoroughly exposed, punished and eliminated. There is no question that these scandals are far too many. This book does not underestimate the evil of these criminal acts. Nevertheless, it is important to search out and uproot the *causes* that have produced and promoted them. I will maintain that these scandals have far deeper **causes** than sexual deviance among celibates and all attempts to conceal and cover them up. These scandals overshadowing the Catholic Church have shaken the faith of so many of the *clean sheep.* Perhaps these terrible scandals may be the necessary wake-up-call for all Christians, especially Catholic Christians to experience a renewal of their faith. It can be a unique moment to discover that authentic faith, hope and charity have a deeper profound understanding than usually understood.

As a newly ordained priest in 1960 returning from studies in Europe I was incapable of understanding the American version of the corrupt clerical culture I was about to enter. It was to take nine difficult years of immersion in this culture. I had to personally experience its mind-sets, its perspectives, its prejudices, and the life-violating consequences of its criminality. Most of all I had to understand the clerical culture within which I was to live. Coming from the open inclusive visions of Vatican Council II, I was a stranger in a very different reality. Yes, without a doubt, in Thomas Merton's expressive words, I had been a timid **guilty by-stander** silent for too many years. I can no longer be so. This **pilgrim's tale** must at last be told. Now is the time. Admittedly for many serious reasons I have hesitated far too long. **I will carry this burden all my life**.

(For it is true that he who is silent does in fact consent.)

Right from the beginning, I had a sense that something unsettling was happening in the Catholic Church clergy caste. Vatican II was definitely not understood. Certainly I was appalled by the lack of understanding I would soon encounter. I was to face the rejection and hostility much like an immigrant from another strange country. I was an outsider whose different way of thinking was a threat to a **normal way** a priest should be, speak and act. As I learned the stories of the priests with whom I began to live and work I was often shocked and offended. As a result of their conversations and behaviors, I came to understand that there was a **cancer** long growing in this clerical culture. This is the reason why their stories must be told. Their stories are true. Many I experienced firsthand. I am a living witness to them. Tragically, as I said, I was also complicit by my silence, a guilty by-stander for too many years. From a perspective of fifty plus years, I am continuously shocked by the scandals that have shaken the Catholic Church today. It is time to shine a spotlight on the unrevealed **fundamental way of thinking and behaving** of these corrupt shepherds. Tragically these scandals have not ended. These stories of priests I encountered in the 1960's are an important part of the history of Catholic priests in the United States. Finally all of the priests in these stories are not named nor should they be. Many are now deceased. Also for anonymity locations and church buildings named as well as nearly all persons named are fictitious. However there are important distinctions that must be made regarding the use of the word *church*. Often in the English language this same word is used to designate very different realities. **Church** may simply mean a building people individually or as a community utilize to practice their particular religious faith. *A **building**, a **church** is* established as a place designed and constructed to assist that practice. The word *church* may also be used to designate inclusively an entire faith based community, as in the **Catholic Church,** the **Congregational Church, etc.** It may also used to refer solely to the leadership or hierarchy of a religious body. For example, the American bishops in their annual council proclaimed a new policy. Thus it may be reported that the **American Church** has spoken. Also it may in some cases refer to the authoritative head of a religious organization itself. So it may be reported that the head of the Russian Orthodox religion has decreed a new doctrine. In the press release it would likely be written The Russian *Church* has finally spoken on this issue of concern. In his letter establishing the Ecumenical Council, to be known as Vatican II, Pope John XXIII **included** in his understanding of **the** *Church* not only the Catholic people and their leaders world-wide today but also the apostles, evangelists, saints, and the myriad of faithful Catholic women and men since the beginning of Christianity. These are **all** *One Holy People of God.* In this book every effort has been to make clear this critical distinction. Here is another. Regarding the sub-title of this book, *Unmasking the true causes of the Scandals in the Catholic Church,* it becomes quite clear that the word **Church** here refers to a significant number of the clergy caste, *the appointed shepherds* among whom are the members of that **corrupt clerical culture** that is the **true cause** of these **long flourishing scandals.** It obviously does not include nor refer to the Catholic Christian people, the clean sheep. Many among them are innocent victims of vicious abuse.

Chapter 1
Newly ordained priest. Home in America. A new life begins.

After four long years in preparation at one of the most venerable and renowned Catholic Universities in Europe, I was ordained a priest. Stepping off the Pan American jet at New York City International Airport I was overjoyed. At the age of 26 I had great expectations. The customs official quickly gave me a down-to-earth moment. He looked at my passport photo and then at me. "My God have you changed!" he said. During my four years away I had lost most of my hair. This would prove to be the least of my problems. "Welcome home Father", he said apologetically but very kindly.

Before returning home to my family I spent the first three weeks after ordination revisiting some of the memorable priests and people I met during my long vacations of four months per year traveling throughout Western Europe. At each stop, there was the celebration of a *First Mass* with a newly ordained priest. There is a strong belief that is especially held in Europe. It is that Catholics who participate in the *First Mass* of a newly ordained priest receive a most special blessing. This is understood as a ticket to heaven. This extraordinary practice has existed for centuries. The places I revisited were:

The Shrine at Lourdes in the French Pyrenees where I had worked for weeks as a chief stretcher bearer directing Irish and English pilgrims from their trains to the several hospitals on the extensive grounds of the shrine. I was given special status because of my ability to speak both French and English. I even wore special insignia designating my necessary position. Often asked, "Did you witness any miracles?" I answered that I had. The miracle I witnessed was this. Very ill pilgrims who had come seeking a miracle for themselves began praying for the healing of someone more seriously ill than they were themselves. I also was part of the taskforce that immersed the sick with great modesty and care into the marble tub of icy waters within the grotto of the shrine while reciting the Hail Mary prayer in French three times. Never did I learn so say that prayer as very rapidly as I did with my arms under that icy water pouring out freely from the rocks above.

Paris, Where I had lived in a parish of worker priests. It was a politely humor filled welcome as my distinct American accent colored my brief sermons. These priests gave me an unforgettable example of what a good shepherd ought to be. They truly lived, labored and suffered together with their sheep.

Rome, St. Peter's in Vatican City where I celebrated Mass at the tomb of the Apostle Peter. Then, together with a small privileged group of newly ordained priests, I had lunch with the jovial Pope John XXIII. Next I toured the Vatican Gardens in the Pope's old brown Mercedes Benz sedan. During the following days I was guided by knowledgeable artists and architects of Vatican City. These many privileges were very unusual as well as insightful learning experiences.

Florence. The parish church overlooking the city to which Dante had fled in exile. I actually slept in the bedroom Dante had occupied centuries before. The pastor, Monsignor G. had graciously welcomed me for two weeks as his young American seminarian guest. To my incredible fortune, he was also a major director of the great Uffizi Art Gallery. Under his tutelage I viewed and studied some of the treasured art of the Renaissance. Most of these were never seen by the average

Chapter 1

tourist. They were housed in special secluded archives in the basement vaults of the gallery. Would my incredible good fortune ever cease? My *First Mass* sermon in American accented book Italian brought laughter to the large assembled congregation of nearly the entire village.

England, The parish church in the village of Westerbury where the pastor had accepted that lost American seminarian, traveling through southern England alone on a three speed bicycle. Proudly he introduced me to some of his famous parishioners. All of them were nuclear physicists working in Great Britain's top secret defense program. Over high tea, that was really a full meal, we engaged in remarkable conversations mostly philosophical and theological. During this *First Mass* sermon, I had no trouble with the language.

Dachau, This horrible concentration camp is 10 miles northwest of Munich. It is near the village where I spent several weeks during two summers. Of all these re-visits in Europe, this, my third visit to Dachau, made the most lasting impact during my remarkable journey. I had wanted never to forget what I had first seen. This was especially true of the well preserved evidence of the Nazi atrocities committed there. It was also the most memorable *First Mass* celebration. I had prepared a brief sermon and memorized the newly ordained priest's blessing in German. I still know it in German. But here it is in English: *May the Blessing of Almighty God, Father, Son and The Holy Ghost descend upon you and forever remain with you. Amen*. At Dachau's newly built chapel, the Carmelite Sisters had gathered a large number of the Hungarian refugees who had fled the 1958 revolution in their homeland. Although the irony perhaps escaped the West German government the refugees were housed in the former concentration camp renovated barracks. Thankfully, like me, these Hungarian people did not speak fluent German. As it turned out we communicated with no difficulty. After the **First Mass** had ended the elderly women and men, one by one, knelt before me for the special new priest's blessing. Immediately, with tears in their eyes they grasped and kissed *my* hands. Tears also filled *my* eyes. As was an ancient custom, I then asked these elderly Catholic people to place their hands on *my* head and bless *me* as I knelt before each one.

> *(As modern scholarship has revealed that early Christian communities actually <u>chose</u> their leaders from within their community and effectually by their choice <u>ordained</u> them to <u>lead</u> the Eucharist celebrations. They followed a practice in Judaism of giving a <u>chosen</u> blessing by the imposition of hands.)*

At that emotional moment something had become very clear to me. As a new priest, I realized it was <u>***I***</u> who owed gratitude not just to The Good Shepherd but also **to the clean sheep, the people of God** who I was ordained to serve. It was a truly life-changing insightful moment. **To this day I have never forgotten the profound meaning of that experience.** It recalls the words St. Augustine spoke as he distributed the Eucharist to each person at Mass. "<u>**You**</u> **are the Body of Christ**!" not "the body of Christ" as is the present practice in the U.S. This distinction has great implications regarding the relationship between the shepherd and his sheep. It will be explored in detail later as this story progresses. Suffice for now to remember that Catholic doctrine holds that **The People of God, Holy Mother Church, The Community of Faithful, We the Holy People**, are also understood in Catholic theology to be **The Mystical Body of Christ. *"Where two or more are gathered in my name, there am I in the midst of them."*** The real presence of the Lord Jesus in His People, *misterium fidei*, the mystery of faith!

My short vacation time was ended due to my **First Mass** farewell celebrations/visits throughout Europe. Within a few days, upon returning to the states, a letter from the bishop's office arrived at my home. It contained my temporary summer assignment. I was to report on the upcoming Saturday to the pastor of a parish in a small picturesque ocean-side town. Here on the east coast these towns often tripled in population during the summer months. So help was needed beyond the Sunday Mass celebrations. That was provided by the usual vacationing priest visitors. Normally a newly ordained priest's summer assignment allowed the pastor to take a long over-due extended vacation.

Chapter 2
The Beginning.
My first assignment as the summer priest.

When I arrived before noon on Saturday the pastor Father Marvin greeted me courteously. We had lunch together served by the chef/secretary. Enticed out of retirement, this kindly woman had been the chef for the Governor of the state. I was immediately impressed, not only by the extraordinary food, but also by the exquisite dinnerware, (double gold rimmed under plates for everything), and also the other lavish appointments of the dining room. This rectory of a small country parish resembled the luxurious living space of an English Manor House. As lunch ended, Father Marvin gave me my assignment. I was to hear confessions that afternoon from 3 to 5 and in the evening from 7 until 9. I would be the only confessor. Regarding Mass on Sunday morning, my duty was to assist vacationing priests who would arrive to celebrate the 7, 8, 9, & 10 a.m. Masses. I was to celebrate the last Mass at 11 a.m. Then Father M. made this astonishing announcement: "Tomorrow, after lunch at 12:30 I will be leaving for an extended vacation. You are to be *on duty alone* during this time. Mrs. Jordan, the chef/secretary would answer any questions you might have. Oh yes, you would have Fridays *off*. I am sure you'll be fine." Then he left without another word. He was obviously accustomed to leaving the *summer priest* on his own. But I must admit I was wordless and quite surprised. There I was left, a totally inexperienced shepherd with a flock as strange to me as I to them.

Saturday afternoon and evening there were very few confessions heard. The *sins* confessed were mostly of the ritual nature. That is they were failures to adhere to rules regarding Mass attendance, Friday meat abstinence, using curse words and little else. Acts of cruelty selfishness, betraying promises, harming relationships with others, ignoring ones personal responsibilities etc., these failures were not considered nor mentioned in this sterile listing of the usual so called *sins*. The Vatican II Council's reforms in attitudes were certainly going to have a very difficult time.

The 3 p.m. confessions ended, I took a brief self-guided tour of the town center. I returned to the rectory. Father Marvin was out so I had to dine alone. Again the dinner was on the level of elegant. Mrs. Jordan was unquestionably a superb chef. When I went out to the kitchen to help with the dishes she gently reminded me that this was not my place. In fact, she would be embarrassed to accept my help. Very gently admonished, I left for confessions to reflect on this day's surprising events.

When I came down to the dining room for breakfast, Father Marvin had already left for the 7 a.m. Mass in the Church next door. There were so few attendees at this early celebration that my assistance was not really needed. So I was to enjoy breakfast and then meet the Sunday visiting priest in the sacristy (vesting room). He would be coming to get properly attired for the 8 a.m. Mass. Each visiting priest was very accustomed to his responsibilities as a Sunday guest celebrant. I had only to assist in the visitor's preparations for Mass and assist with distributing communion. I was kept busy because the next Mass followed only fifteen minutes later. The routine was well known to these yearly vacationing priests. They usually declined breakfast preferring to return with their families to their summer cottages. These were often more substantial and expensive homes

Chapter 2

on the nearby beaches. Cottages they were surely not. They were often owned, I later learned, by the priest of the family himself.

I was left quite alone to celebrate the 11 o clock Mass. This turned out to be the most populated celebration of the day. That first Sunday my sermon developed the Gospel message: *Love thy neighbor as thyself*. I sensed that my emphasis on the importance of *loving and respecting oneself* being an all important factor in **loving** *thy neighbor* was not the usual perspective. The renewal of the Catholic Church being advocated by Vatican Council was asking Catholics to emphasize their goodness and dignity as *God's holy people.* This way of thinking about themselves would run up against a long held ideology among most Catholics. This strongly emphasized guilt, fear and sinfulness. For nearly all Catholics everywhere, not only Americans, these elements together with a profound **unworthiness** were deeply instilled by means of early childhood persistent instructions. Of course this included the great honor, respect and even veneration always to be had for the priest. The priest often claimed and in many cases, truly believed he himself was the very spokesperson of God on earth. He actually believed that he was by ordination far superior to the people the lay women and men he was appointed to protect and serve.

And shame it is if a priest the shepherd among his innocent sheep betray his promises, he is then a corrupt hypocritical unclean shepherd for his sheep.

> *(This excerpt taken from The Canterbury Tales is translated here into contemporary less colorful but still forceful English.)*

As Mass ended, it occurred to me that I should not simply walk into the vesting room behind the sanctuary as was customary. Rather I should walk down the center aisle and position myself at the door of the church to greet the people as they left. This was a practice I had experienced in the worker-priest parish of St. Vincent in Paris where I had lived for several weeks. However it was not usual in Catholic Parishes in the U.SA. But it *was* quite customary in non-Catholic and other weekend religious celebrations. I was greeted by great surprise. This was also accompanied by warm handshakes, smiles, and the words, **glad to meet you Father.** It seemed to be a very good beginning.

Late that first Sunday afternoon came my first emergency. The State Police called to report that an officer would arrive any minute to take the parish priest to a serious accident on the nearby Interstate. Someone was badly injured and asked for a priest. Gathering my never before used last rites packet, I had hardly made it to the front door when the officer arrived, car out front, motor running, lights flashing. We drove to the scene of the accident at speeds exceeding 90 mph. We were too late. The driver, an elderly man had been found dead as reported by the first responders already on site. The deceased was bent behind the wheel of the late model luxury car that had stopped against the guard rail. In the passenger's seat was the man's wife sobbing inconsolably. Through her tears she said, "We had been to the doctor's office only yesterday. He had a heart condition but all the test results were fine". She paused to thank me. Then she watched quietly as I proceeded to anoint her dead husband's forehead and recite the prayers for the dead. Again she expressed her gratitude for my presence. It was my first experience as a priest, up close with the finality of death. On the way back to the rectory I rode in thoughtful silence. I knew so little. Academic studies were no substitute for life's reality. As was insightfully written, "Life is **difficult…**and it is **supposed** to be".

(The Road Less Traveled written by M. Scott Peck makes this very clear.)

Chapter 3
First encounter with the entrenched clerical culture.

It became quite clear that "being on duty" had very restrictive consequences. Here in the 1960's with very limited communication technology, *being on duty* meant a priest must be always accessible lest someone be about to die or is already dead. This restriction applied to me, the sole *summer priest* alone in my assigned parish. In addition nearby parishes borrowed the services of the *summer priest* to be on duty in their parishes as well. Also the *summer priest* was often requested to hear confessions at the conclusions of nearby parish's special events called *missions*. Compliance with any such request was always expected. In this summer assignment I faced my first odious encounter with a long standing practice in the clerical culture. This was payment in cash for doing priestly duties. So, when requested, I responded. This entailed the hearing of confessions, the sacrament of forgiveness. Such symbols of Christ's love for His people had, over centuries, developed within the clerical culture a complex price schedule. Was it any wonder that Martin Luther revolted against the price structure so dominant in his time. At the top of this price schedule was this phenomenal creation. It was given only by the Pope. This so called **plenary papal indulgence was a full pardon for a sinful life**. It engendered a specific price well beyond the capability of a poor Catholic layman (**Chaucer's** *lewd man*). This together with countless *lesser benefits* continues to this day. The encounter with this payment structure for exercising my duties as a priest came very early. The clerical culture had prescribed a specific price for every priestly official function. There was **nothing** without a cost. This was true not only for benefits in this life but extended beyond the grave to the Middle Age theological **construct** commonly known as *purgatory*. To better understand the centuries old corrupt clerical culture the contemporary admonitions *follow the money* is most appropriate. It was only a few days after the call to the accident on the Interstate that a request was made to spend that Thursday evening hearing confessions at the conclusion of a week-long summer *mission* being held in a nearby parish. Arriving early, I found myself in the rear of the church building listening to the concluding sermon. The audience was composed **entirely** of elderly people, mostly women. The preacher was denouncing the terrible sins of abortion and birth control. As he spoke he stood in the pulpit embracing a large black wooden cross. This was a common practice among members of his religious community when conducting such a *mission.* The message was clearly designed to elicit *fear and trembling.* Compassion, empathy, and forgiveness, had no place in it. As the evening's session ended, I retired to the sole confessional. There for over an hour I listened to the usual ritual failures of missing prayers, being away from confession too long and being late for Mass on Sundays. All these came at me through the screen. It goes without saying that the *great sins* the preacher had so vehemently denounced were totally absent from this recitation. My novice attempts to promote an understanding of Christ's message of loving compassion toward the sinner were futile. In this historical context how could it be otherwise? When the last penitent left, I returned to the rectory to say good night. There in the living room was the pastor and the preacher of the *mission* enjoying a relaxing conversation over some alcoholic beverages and cigars. Although attempting to make a polite departure the command was immediately given to sit and join us in a drink. Forgoing the scotch and cigars, I sat and had a coffee instead. The conversation continued with the preacher commenting on his perceived great success of his financially profitable *mission*. He proclaimed, "I really had them convinced that birth control was

Chapter 3

a horrible sin. Like abortion, it was destroying the gift of life itself. No true Catholic could ever excuse these offenses." He and the pastor continued to reinforce one another regarding these evils. They were convinced that these parishioners needed to hear this message. They seemed oblivious to the fact that the attendees of the *mission* were very elderly people long past the childbearing age.

I rose to leave. The pastor followed me out to the front walk where he pressed a twenty dollar bill into my hand. "This is for helping us" he said with a smile. Protesting I said I could not accept payment for my duties. He snarled, "You have a lot to learn young man. Don't you dare insult me like this". With that, he turned and left me standing there. Still clutching the 20 dollar bill, I got into my car and drove back to the rectory. The road less traveled was going to be more difficult than I had ever expected. I placed the $20 in the locked box for donations to the poor at the rear of door of my summer church. That pastor was right. I did have a lot to learn far more than he could ever understand...

(Many years later, I was to learn the mission preacher and members of his community were exposed as predators of children. They were truly in biblical terms, whitened sepulchers filled with dead men's bones. Later Pope Francis would be quoted regarding these pedophiles: "Millstones should be placed upon their necks and they should be dropped into the depths of the sea.")

The 11 o'clock Sunday Mass began to be filled beyond capacity. Word had spread to nearby towns that the *new priest* was worth hearing. Even some of the vacationing priests would remain in the vesting room to listen to my sermons. The messages about a possible renewal in Catholic thinking, especially in the area of sexual morality, were falling like welcome rain on parched earth. There was especially a great curiosity concerning the possibility of explicit change in the regulations concerning birth control. Requests by married couples for private conferences as well as talks with the summer study groups in neighboring parishes and even guest speaker engagements by civic groups all began to fill my evening calendar. The family planning decisions facing American Catholics were placing extraordinary burdens on every aspect of their lives. Each and everyone I met wanted to live as faithful practicing Catholics. However the choices imposed upon them by the teachings of Catholic Church doctrine, as it was dictated to them by the clerical caste and as they understood it, was immensely disturbing. This church doctrine just did not match up with the reality of their lives. Therefore the news that the "**Church**" was *changing* presented to ordinary Catholic people **hope writ large.** So I was asked over and over again, "Is it true as you have preached that Vatican Council II was going to rethink some of the most oppressive regulations? Is it true that the breakthrough in scientific methods of birth control might become acceptable? Is it true that Pope John XXIII has commissioned a task force composed of clergy *and* lay people, men *and* women, moral theologians **and** scientists, doctors **and** lawyers who are people from all parts of the world? Is it true that the Pope has said he will consult with them, listen to them, and **take their recommendations** on the issue of birth control **seriously?** Is this all true?" The next eight weeks were not going to be spent in just thoughtful silence after all. Instead there was much mutual learning to explore.

Two of these invitations to speak on the potential changes in church teaching turned out to be revealing. A major one came from the editors of a popular Catholic magazine. It was an invitation to speak to editors, reporters and staff of this journal. I was to be a newly published contributor of the magazine. While at the University in Europe, I had sent an article on the proposal being considered by Vatican II regarding permitting national churches to celebrate Mass in the *vernacular.* This would mean **using the language of the people** instead of the traditional Latin. In the article, I had questioned the centuries old practice of disparaging the vast majority of Catholic people (**the laypeople**). It was employing a language used mostly by the elite clerical caste. It had become clear to a large number of European Catholic theologians that this exclusivity was the antithesis of the **inclusivity** at the heart of Christianity. Moreover, this separate and unequal status, denounced by St. Paul in the earliest Christian communities, should have no part among God's Holy People. The practice of **an elite exclusive language** in the communal act of worship should not be undermining the Christian message of inclusivity. **Inclusivity** was precisely at the core of Vatican II's message of renewal,

Using my F*riday off,* I took the train to the metropolitan center to meet with the editors and staff of the journal that would publish my article. The eagerness to hear about the changes regarding birth control was evident. I gave them what information I had learned from some of my professors. These theologians had gone to Rome as advisors to their own bishops. But their message was complex and uncertain. Our conversation focused upon those Catholic couples faced with seemingly irreconcilable choices. The current prohibitions imposed by Catholic moral teaching regarding human sexuality were creating crises of guilt and suffering.

*(The so called **Catholic Russian roulette**, the rhythm method, was, in years to come, discovered to be truly an **unnatural practice** that was **destroying** marital relationships. Unfortunately this truth was not known to us during our meeting in 1962. Also most sadly Pope John XXIII would be dead after the first full year of Vatican II. The potential solutions would depend on the new pope's decisions.)*

The managing editor asked the most critical question. It proved to be very perceptive. "Would the Secretary of State, the known arch-conservative and highly influential Cardinal Alfredo Ottaviani, **allow** any Pope including Pope John XXIII to overrule the pronouncements of the majority of his predecessors?"

We asked would this powerful Cardinal threaten the Pope with undermining the pronouncements of the previous century's Vatican Council I? That Council had stated that in matters of faith and **morals** the Pope is **infallible**! But if he, the Pope reversed Catholic doctrine on sexuality would he destroy all papal credibility severely overturning this key doctrine? These were the critical questions that we all knew had to be answered. But none of us in that meeting in the early 60's had any of the answers. How could we have?

> *(After years of anguished hesitation, countless meetings and speculation, not only in the Vatican II deliberations but in schools of theology world-wide, the answer finally came after these six long years of procrastination. It arrived like a category seven earth quake. In 1968 Pope Pau VI who had succeeded Pope John XIII published his encyclical letter entitled Humanae Vita (of Human Life). It completely ignored the tentative proposals of Vatican II as well as the advice of the advisory board of scholarly lay people, some bishops and their theologians. The encyclical proclaimed that the prohibitions against all forms of artificial birth control were to remain in force for all Catholics. Only years later did research uncover that the powerful Cardinal Ottaviani together with the band of clerics known as the Pope's administrators, the Roman Curia, had prevailed. In 1870 nearly 100 years to the day of Humanae Vitae, the British representative to Vatican Council I, John Henry Cardinal Newman strongly had warned that this pronouncement declaring papal infallibility would bring*

Chapter 3

about great misfortune and false interpretations. In the 20th century this had become unfortunately and tragically true. It is remarkable that in 2019, John Henry Cardinal Newman, was declared a saint of the Catholic Church. The arrogant autocratic Cardinal Alfredo Ottavianni and the indecisive Hamlet-like Pope Paul VI, now both long deceased, surely would have opposed naming Cardinal Newman a saint of the entire Catholic Church.)

Leaving the meeting with the people of the Catholic Journal I could not stop thinking of all I had learned. There was so much. The major insight was a flash-like ***whack on the side of the head.*** The intellectual theological approach to the birth control issue was **inadequate** and **even unrealistic**. My attempts to offer a solution that placed the birth control decisions dealing with the complex spectrum of choices faced by each couple **directly upon they themselves** did not help at all. The prohibitions decreed by the *administration* of the Catholic Church were not easily set aside by the consciences of devout practicing Catholics. The cost in anxiety and guilt was far too great. I was beginning to awaken to the truth: **I had no sense of the difficulty a married couple faced should they *go against* the regulations of their church's doctrine.** The sense that I really had no experience, no existential knowledge of the married Catholic's life was overwhelming. More to the point it was deeply humbling and **profoundly disturbing**. It would take me a long time and deep personal reflection to realize this profound truth. **There is not an easy progression from the intellectual grasp of the concept to the emotional acceptance of it.** There is a growth process that is psychologically difficult for each person. It cannot be rushed. I still had so much to learn. A good friend from Ireland put this understanding forcefully when he told me: "**You see young man there is quite a difference between a horse chestnut and a chestnut horse**"

(I can still hear him saying in his strong Irish accent: glory to God, there truly is!)

Returning to my summer assignment a disturbing surprise awaited me. It was the first Sunday of August just after the 8 a.m. Mass when the visiting celebrant approached me with the news. He showed me his copy. My article in the Catholic Journal had been published. What had been a section of my proposed doctoral thesis and had initiated my visit to the publishers meeting was becoming a national sensation. There on the front cover in large bold print was the title **Renewal in the Church** with my name in equally bold print as its author. Together with his congratulations the visiting priest asked, "How did you get the bishop's permission for this big story?" I had submitted the article while still in Europe and received a letter of acceptance one month before I had left. In my political naivety and youthful ignorance of clerical culture authoritarian regulations I had never thought it necessary to ask the bishop's permission. The staff of the Journal had noted that my article would be published very soon but no date was given. Was I in some serious trouble already? That morning also came my good fortune. The Mass at 10 was celebrated by the priest who was the editor of the Diocesan Catholic weekly newspaper. He too congratulated me and assured me that he and the bishop were pleased at my success. My good fortune was to prove a benefit to the diocese in the months to come. For the time being, my article focusing on the inclusivity of worship through language was to be a ***must read*** for all those hundreds participating in the National Liturgical Conference. This conference would be focusing precisely on Catholics throughout the world using the **vernacular**, their own language, **in every act of worship**. It was to be held in Chicago at the end of the month. Most unfortunately, although invited, my responsibilities as the ***summer priest*** made attendance completely out of the question.

Chapter 4
Difficulties with the clerical culture intensifies.

My summer assignment was fast approaching its end. I was surprised to learn that many parishioners had jointly written a letter petitioning the bishop to make a notable exception. They had asked him to make permanent my summer assignment. Without doubt my sermons, personal conferences with many parishioners, and numerous family study club visits in these few weeks had a profound impact. Nevertheless, this extraordinary request was accepted but firmly denied. Father Marvin was due to return early on Friday morning of the upcoming weekend. Days before the letter with my new assignment arrived. I was to report on that very Friday to Father Anton Vittor, the pastor of the renovated Church of St. Hilary. The oldest church of the diocese was located in the center of the city of Adamsburgh, the State Capitol.

With a tearful sad goodbye to Mrs. Jordan and a formal hand-shake with a thank you for your services parting from Father Marvin I left my joyful first assignment before noon that Friday. The drive to St. Hilary rectory was uneventful but filled with expectations. I had done some research regarding my new assignment. I was to have a dual role, both as the new junior curate (new priest) as well as Ph.D. professor of Ethics and Religious Studies at the Catholic College of St. Thomas Aquinas. This was one of a number of colleges that comprised Adamsburgh University. All of these colleges were located within the Capitol City on a large sprawling campus. My meeting with the Academic Dean to introduce myself was not until Monday, but the meeting with the pastor, Father Vittor, was to be that Friday afternoon at 3 o'clock. Arriving on time at the rectory door, I was met by Lucy, the house-keeper. "Welcome Father, we have been expecting you" she greeted me with a pleasant smile. She told me that the pastor would receive me in his office on the second floor. I should wait until he summoned me. After several minutes he told Lucy to send me to him. This was not exactly the greeting I had expected. However his reputation as a somewhat stern man had been accurate. I remember clearly that his office door was closed. Upon my soft knock came the single word "Enter". So began my introduction to my new assignment. Father Vittor did not mince words. His opening sentence I will never forget. "You will be of little use to us here. I asked for a junior assistant and the chancery has sent me a part time curate and a full time teacher." With no acknowledgement for my responsibilities as a college professor, he proceeded to spell out my duties as he had determined them. "You are to celebrate 11 a.m. Mass every Sunday but also assist with the distribution of communion at the 7 8, 9 and 10 o'clock Masses. Hear confessions every Saturday from 3 to 5 p.m. and 7 to 9 p.m. On many Saturdays you may be the only confessor. Be on duty at least two weeks per month. As the priest from St. Hilary be at every wake held for this National Parish no matter how far it may be within the greater Adamsburgh area. When on duty, be responsible for conducting all Sunday Baptisms scheduled or unscheduled between 1 and 2 p.m. Deliver communion to the home-bound on the first Friday of every month wherever their homes may be in the greater area of this national parish. And finally, though a very small in number of participants you are in charge of the CYO (Catholic Youth Organization) meeting every Monday evening. Regarding the scheduling of Funerals, whenever your class schedule at the college allows, you will serve as only the sub-deacon never the celebrant. Finally the parish secretary will give you a written copy of all of these duties lest you forget them. If there are any questions, the two senior curates will answer them. Your suite of rooms is on the third floor. Manage your belongings yourself.

Chapter 4

There are no elevators." He ended his pronouncements with the words "You're dismissed".

That evening, before and after dinner, I was to have some time meeting with the two senior curates. The older, John Mitchell was cordial, helpful and most amiable. The younger, Andy Vainer seemed to take his lead from the pastor. He evidently shared the view that rather a helpmate, I was more a burden. John began by giving me an in depth understanding of the history and implications of this ***National Parish***.

Here is what I learned. The large one-spire Church of St. Hilary was indeed the oldest Catholic Church in Adamsburgh. Located just one block west of the city-center, the parish was now in the midst of the commercial area. The area was filled with large department stores, hotels, restaurants, and office buildings. While it had once been in the center of an extensive up-scale residential section of the city, St. Hilary community had long ago lost all its parishioners to the suburbs. To make matters worse, six years ago a devastating fire had extensively ruined the interior of the beautiful old church building. On either side, and closely connected to it, flames and falling objects from the fire had severely damaged the rectory, elementary school and convent But great as this tragedy was, a final blow was about to descend.

Father Henry the pastor of St. Hilary was a respected icon of the clergy. Honored by the previous bishop of the diocese, he had been named a Monsignor. In the Roman Catholic clerical culture he now held the office of domestic prelate, not quite a bishop, a.k.a. Monsignor. He was also special advisor to the Bishop of the Diocese. This reward not only honored the priest but the special position or parish in which he served. Unfortunately the great fire at St. Hilary revealed that Monsignor Henry the mysteriously retired pastor had for more than 30 years never paid the thousands of dollars each year in property fire insurance premiums. Though listed in the church records as always paid, Monsignor Henry had been secretly embezzling the insurance premiums in order to purchase a luxurious Caribbean home for his retirement.

> 𝔉or if a preest be foul on whom we truste, 𝔑o wonder is a lewed man to ruste…𝔄 shitten shepherde and a clene sheep.
> -The Canterbury Tales, Prologue II.

> *(For if a priest be corrupt in whom we trust, No wonder is a poor layman to be sinful. A shitten shepherd and a clean sheep.)*

According to the precepts of the clerical culture, this scandal had to be swiftly kept hidden. Monsignor Henry was **taken ill and retired and never seen nor heard from again.** The tale of arrogance, greed, entitlement and crime was never publically revealed. **Situation Normal**! The well established practice of *cover-it-up* was efficiently employed.

> *(Only the bishop's team knew the details of the scandal. But after a time the news got out. Then it spread like a wild fire throughout the Adamsburgh clergy caste. The disappearance was so complete as if Monsignor Samuel Henry had never existed.)*

Father John continued the hidden story of St. Hilary the only **National Parish** in the diocese. How did the diocese restore St. Hilary's Church building, build a new rectory, a renewed elementary school and a new convent with no funds available? The bishop, together with his advisors, the members of his chancery office, (his inner circle, and the governing mechanism of the clerical culture of the diocese) had developed a very creative solution. It was complex. But all the parts finally came together.

Chapter 4

The diocese at the time of the tragic fire owned a very large parcel of land east of the center of the capitol city. It was considered the poorest section of Adamsburgh. In its midst was the parish of St. Theresa. It was most likely that its parishioners would soon be leaving and hopefully employed in the huge new automobile assembly plant being constructed several miles south of the city. The original plan for the diocese was to build a new St. Theresa's church building near the new plant. Father Vittor was to continue as pastor of this parish community of largely multi-ethnic emigrant working class Catholics. As an incentive for the move the new plant's ownership had offered to help subsidize the cost of a large area of well subsidized moderate cost housing together with a new church building, a large supermarket etc. In fact it would be a company owned community. Now the final piece of the bishop's creative solution was miraculously about to materialize.

The city's oldest fortune five hundred company's real estate division proposed to purchase for an immense sum that large parcel of diocesan owned land. On it they planned to construct a magnificent architecturally stunning office complex. It would be the crown jewel of the city and the state. For the bishop and his team, this was truly **manna come down from heaven.** And so it came to pass, the parishioners of St. Theresa had a new modern style church building plus a new young and perhaps a more kindly pastor. But for these mostly first generation immigrants the best news of all was the much needed new affordable housing. In addition, there was already close by a newly built public grammar school with easy transition to any of the cities three high schools.

The interior of St. Hilary Church building was restored, accompanied by a newly renovated elementary school, a new convent and a new enlarged rectory able to accommodate a staff of four resident parish priests as well as three priests who held special positions in the diocesan bureaucracy. To complete the picture was this final enhancement. St. Hilary's Catholic Church community, not having a base of parishioners, would become a **special *National Parish.*** This meant that ***any*** Catholic, actively practicing or **not**, but still a baptized Catholic, could use all the services of St. Hilary Church parish community. This enabled their children to be students of St. Hilary Catholic elementary school free of charge, access all baptisms, weddings, and funerals. In addition the service of the parish priest at wakes, burials, hospital visits, and the administration of all the sacraments. ***The only requirement*** was to be a Catholic resident within the greater Adamsburgh area. This included occupants of hotels, hospital patients, temporary visiting residents of the city and all rest homes. In greater Adamsburgh the parish community of St. Hilary would become **everybody's** Catholic parish! Most importantly, there were to be **no questions ever asked** regarding anyone being a practicing or non-practicing Catholic. In the past this **inquisition** had been a stumbling block for many lapsed and divorced Catholics. Finally the pastor of St. Hilary parish city-wide community was now Father Anton Vittor.

Then Father John began to explain the unwritten rules that governed the relationship between the pastor, and his three assistants.

Rule one: His behavior might often appear to be narcissistic, autocratic and cruel. **It often was.** He was still the *boss*. His assistants must **never** forget this. He was sure to award their loyal subservience with the many financial rewards that were within his power to bestow. They were very available in a National Parish with so many weddings, funerals and other benefits. These were never explicitly described as *payments* but euphemistically known in the corrupt clerical culture as *stipends*. **These are the fees collected for ordinary priestly duties.**

Chapter 4

(To understand what is really happening in most criminal enterprises it is wise always to just follow the money!)

Here is a listing. The *stipend* schedule for a solemn (three priest) funeral was distributed as follows: $25 for the use of the church, $25 for the celebrant, $10 for the deacon, and $5 for the sub-deacon. The funeral directors would add these costs to their total funeral fee. Father Vittor always assigned all the funerals to his assistants. On average there were four funerals per week. All funerals of the homeless poor of the area were state contracted with designated undertakers. All were to be held at St. Hilary. Every memorial *high Mass* noted in the daily paper was $25 ($20 for the celebrant and $5 for the organist). Special donations by funeral directors to St. Hilary for having a priest at the burial sites and at wakes were understood. Small specially marked envelopes distributed at every Sunday Mass as well as available in the rectory office gave assured remembrance of the deceased loved one whose soul may still be suffering in *purgatory*. Two dollars should be placed in these together with the deceased's name. These many envelopes would be bound together and placed on the altar during every Mass for one month. All proceeds were undisclosed of course. Remarkably, there was a precise schedule of **stipends** and their specific *price* for everything. This included all Weddings: $50 use of the church, $25 for the celebrant, $20 to the organist, $20 if used for the vocalist.

All distributions to the church treasury and to the priests of St. Hilary were carefully managed by the pastor. It was assumed, but not known with certainty, that all these financial records were kept secretly and securely in the basement vault. There was never an audit conducted nor any financial statement published. *Situation Normal!* All was under Father Vittor's sole non accountability control.

And so it goes. If he quietly obeyed the rules, an assistant of St. Hilary could augment his salary of $200 per month by hundreds of dollars **per**

week. I, the so described *useless assistant,* was not a beneficiary of this highly profitable secretive corrupt clerical practice,

> And shame it is, if a preest take keep- shitten shepherds and clene sheep.

> *(And shame it is, if a priest betray his promises, shitten shepherds and clean sheep.)*

Rule two: Never mention the luxuriousness of the food. The *boss* had made financial arrangements with several of the local restaurants. They would take turns each for one week at a time sending their nightly specials to the priest's table. Lucy did not prepare dinner or even lunch. Lunch was always a variety of cold cuts cheeses salads and breads. All were brought in by local delicatessens. The contents of the meals were very tasteful but hardly a weight-watchers diet. Lucy did make breakfast as well as keep the schedule of priests who would be present for each meal. She maintained the refrigerator fully supplied with an abundance of leftovers and deserts. Dining at St. Hilary was five stars. It was fitting for the *gents* (as American priests privately called themselves). Nothing was ever too good for these *gentlemen* of the corrupt clerical culture.

> *(Will it never end? Lasting for so many centuries it seems likely it will ever remain unless the necessary radical elimination of the corrupt clerical culture in its entirety takes place.)*

Rule three: Never inquire what the *boss* was doing every Sunday afternoon in the specially constructed vault-room in the basement. In fact, never ask about the vault-room at all. Only the parish secretary and the *boss* had the combination to the safe-like large steel door. There was much speculation regarding its contents, but no one really knew. No rectory resident dared ask. It was to be just a *mystery of faith.*

Chapter 4

So Father John repeatedly emphasized that the benefits as an assistant at St Hilary far outweighed any difficulties one might have. He said most priests of this diocese would relish the opportunity to be an assistant there. Besides the money, the pastor never questioned the use of one's **time off** or how an assistant used his **financial rewards**. In these matters his policy was never to mention it.

> *(The ancient adage ruled: to keep silent is to consent. As it was explained to Henry VIII's criminal court by St. Thomas Moore centuries past when defending his silence. He was suggesting that it should be used to establish his consent to the king's marriage. Therefore by law Thomas Moore could uphold his innocence. In a like manner Father Vittor give his silent stamp of approval to the behavior of his subservient loyal assistants. He doubtlessly believed he was innocent of their extracurricular behaviors.)*

My first Saturday night when confessions were over I experienced this policy directly. As the senior assistant, John occupied the largest suite of rooms on the third floor of the rectory. It included a very large living room where John's priest friends would gather once per month for a convivial party after hearing confessions on Saturday evenings. Not public knowledge was an unwritten long standing rule stating: ***priests should not be out at night after having heard confessions.*** This was to ensure that no appearance of scandal regarding possible sexual assignations might have been made during women's confessions. So the monthly Saturday night party at St. Hilary was a well kept secret. As the newly arrived assistant, I was invited in hopes that I might become a member of this very secret club meeting. John and Andy had left the confessionals quite early to set up John's living room with food and drinks. Left behind to lock up, I was the last to arrive. The party was well underway. Friendly introductions were made amidst jovial and somewhat animated conversations now being fueled by the alcoholic beverages abundantly available. After a short time, the main event of the evening took place. Two of John's friends, actual classmates of ten years past, had recently returned from vacation at a resort well known for its luxurious status. Andy set up a projector. The two priests proceeded to show a film of them engaging in explicit sexual activity with several of the women they had **befriended** during their trip. The group being well distracted by this pornography, I quietly slipped out thoroughly shocked offended and embarrassed.

Subsequently, I discovered that this was a very common occurrence at these gatherings. In place of films, explicit photographs of such exploits were much more commonly viewed and freely shared. Sometimes even special **befriended** guests were invited as well.

For if a prest be foul on whom we truste....

John alone noticed that I had left. Sensing what I felt, he pleaded with me to keep the existence of these parties secret. I promised I would keep silent. Until now I have. Regarding the identity of any participants I have never revealed any identity of the priests who took part. I never will.

(I subsequently learned that the club parties like the ones at St. Hilary were held in many rectories in many dioceses throughout the United States. These parties were often known as Wisconsin Club meetings. Wisconsin true meaning -<u>We can sin.</u> But I remained silent for so many years.. I can never forget to my shame that to remain silent can often be interpreted as to consent.)

Chapter 5
The joy of helping others learns that God has created all of us in His Own *image*.

The Monday meetings in preparation for my teaching proved to be more positive than the encounter with Father Vittor. The College Dean, Dr. Robert Shaw, was as welcoming as he could be. Most important among everyone I met at the college was the Catholic Chaplin of the University. Father Seven Harrison. He and I immediately found one another on common ground regarding the current needs of the entire Catholic Church. Our hope was they were now finally going to be addressed by Pope John XXIII in calling for this Ecumenical Council meeting in Vatican City. It was to consist of all the Cardinals, bishops, theologians, and laymen scholars from every part of the world. It was to be known as Vatican II. Its mandate in the words of Pope John XXIII **was to** *open the windows of the Church and let in fresh air.* In the 1960's *change* was decidedly in the air. The first Catholic American President had declared that *the torch has been past to a new generation, born in this century.*

It was timely that Father Steven, just appointed by the bishop as first Catholic Chaplin at Adamsburgh University, should bring together a group of recently ordained knowledge-seeking young priests. Their goal was to learn what Vatican II might really be all about. So on the last Monday of September we met for the very first time. We hoped to share our understandings drawn from what we had read and heard about this renewal. What was this *fresh air* blowing through the perhaps *stagnant air* of the entire Church? Exactly what would this *renewal* mean for the two thousand year old Catholic Church we had known since our earliest years? Very specifically, what would it mean for *us* the latest group of newly appointed *shepherds?*

After a brief get to know one another session, our conversations began with a multitude of questions. The list was long and diverse. It included the issue of celibacy, women's role in the Church community and much more. This was especially true of the concept of **inclusivity** regarding the laymen, other Christian faiths, the Jewish faith and other major faiths as well. There were also the questions brought about by advancements in biblical scholarship together with the radical changes in worship practices as well as certain prohibitions. *Above all it was the issue of birth control!*

Father Steve had introduced me as one who had recently returned from Europe and could provide some valuable information. Listening to the questions and comments both explicit and inferred I was especially aware that the letter of warning given to the Pope at the very beginning of Vatican II:

Beware Holy Father, the vast majority of the clergy are totally unprepared to understand and, more importantly, to accept the changes the Ecumenical Council was considering. (*Signed the Austrian Bishops delegation*)

As I attempted to answer some of their questions, our conversations revealed a mind-set conditioned by years of prejudices misconceptions myths superstitions and definite falsehoods. Many questions were a collection of biblical misinterpretations, literal interpretations of stories that were intended to be symbolic. It was as if the writings and traditions of Christianity were all recorded on *video tape*. Theological historical investigations of biblical scholarship published

Chapter 5

31

by the theology schools in the Universities of Europe all seemed to have hardly any influence in the education of American priests. Certainly none had reached the priests in this group. The task before me appeared to be truly impossible. There was an analogy that I had used in my journal article. I had hoped this might soften the impact on their ***world view***. I knew that my explanations were sure to threaten it. This is how I began.

All of us have used the word *sincere* many times. But its origin has a colorful history dating back to ancient Rome. Expensive vases were often made of clay but beautifully painted and adorned with precious gems. They were sometimes accidently broken. Unscrupulous merchants had discovered that using simple wax (***cera*** in Latin) they could glue a broken vase back together. Then, undetected, sell it as new. But clever wealthy Romans would always test every expensive vase by exposing it to the heat of the Roman sun. If it remained intact then it was not held together by wax. It was without wax ***sina-cera (in Latin) (in English sincere)***. The vase was indeed authentic, i.e., ***sincere***. One could buy it with confidence at the asking price. Now back to explaining the Ecumenical Council, Vatican II. Clearly Pope John XXIII wanted the Council to open the windows of the Catholic Church teachings and practices. The task would be to examine and to change some of these tightly held positions, practices and restrictions. He believed many greatly needed the breath of fresh air and warm bright sunlight that Vatican II would bring. Was it possible that the "*wax*" that had been holding together some of these well intentioned unfortunate errors might just melt and be blown away? I had hoped this preamble might pave the way for what was to come. **It did not**

Then I gave what I thought might be two clarifying examples. Accredited biblical linguistic scholars had discovered that some books in the bible begin with the words, "*once upon a time, in a land far away*". Would they then believe the book before them was an actual well researched historical work truly factual? Most assuredly they would not. They would realize this was a brilliantly written, *symbolic, creative and meaningful narrative.* In fact, these scholars clearly understood they were examining a magnificent *novel, a truly a great work of fiction.* With these very words, the thought provoking *novel begins.* But these opening words do not appear in any popular translation of the *Book of Job.* They can only be discerned by recognizing the stylistic formats of the ancient Hebrew writings. It takes much study and expertise to comprehend ancient Hebrew texts. Those who espouse a strict literal interpretation of an English Bible will find themselves in a world of continuous misinterpretations. The second example has even more serious consequences.

In 312 A.D., Emperor Constantine made Christianity the official state religion of the Roman Empire. Constantine left Rome and established his rule from the East in the new capital of the Empire he named Constantinople (*today Istanbul*). The Bishop of Rome, the Pope, was left on his own in the greatly threatened western empire's former capitol city. Emperor Constantine wished to encourage the Pope in some way. He granted him in a written decree, *all the islands* of the river Tiber that was flowing through the city of Rome. In the fifth century nearly 100 years later, trying to please the contemporary Pope, his own document scribes deliberately changed the above mentioned decree from "*all the islands of the Tiber (Tiberium)* **to** *all the islands of the Empire(Tiberium is easily morphed into Emperium by using a clever illuminative writing style.*

This is the importance. From that time and continuing for many centuries, Popes claimed to own all the *islands* of the Holy Roman Empire. They then taxed their rulers together with all the people who lived on those *islands.* Among them were the islands of the Mediterranean and most importantly the islands of Great Britain including and especially Ireland. In the discoveries of Columbus, all the i*slands* he discovered

Chapter 5

were made in the name of the Holy Roman Catholic Church ruled by the Pope and in the name of the Kingdom of Spain then ruled by its King and Queen the powerful Ferdinand and Isabella. This included all the *islands* of the western hemisphere including all the Caribbean Islands, as well as the vast countries of Mexico, Central and South America. (All were considered by Columbus and his successors to be *islands*.)

Is it any wonder that Henry VIII was able to convince most of the people of Great Britain to separate from Rome and the foreign Pope? They already resented Popes for taxing them? So from a **T** to an **E** the Reformation in the British Islands had fertile ground in which to grow. The impact of that fifth century important but long unrevealed *changed document* has continued into our time. I asked our group how many of us have ever had friendly conversations with the Church of England members, or *any* Episcopalian clergymen. Augmenting the question I asked, "Had we ever had *any* conversations with *any* of the Christian clergy in greater Adamsburgh?" **Silence that speaks so loudly answered my request**.

For many in our group my logical historical intellectual explanations could not deal with the *large elephants in the room*. Their questions continued to be deeply troubling. Did Vatican II's changes mean that what we had long believed about so much of our faith is false so no longer valid? Had we been misled by the leaders we always trusted? Had we then misled so many Catholic people who admired us, listened to us and trusted us? The Canterbury Tales in Prologue II is given a somewhat different version:

> If the shepherd be misled, in whom we truste,
> No wonder is the poor sheep to ruste.

They were really asking, "Are we to accept that: 1) our Catholic faith had been in a state of evolution since its very origins? 2) Disputes many even violent, had existed among the early Christian communities? 3) so many of our traditions and practices were not immutable but subject to continuous developme4nt perfectibility and even radical change or elimination? Have we been so wrong for so long?" Did I dare tell them the answer to all their questions is a definite **yes**! It was time for them to face the truth. Analogously, the clergy in Galileo's time ought to have believed the evidence of his discovery that the earth is not flat but round, truly a sphere. These young clergymen ought now to face the solid historical evidence that Christianity has evolved from its beginnings and is continuing to do so. For the priests in Father Steve's group this was not going to happen any time soon, if at all. Steve and I knew not what was coming.

*(Would it take these great ongoing scandals in the Catholic Church- the sexual violation of the innocent together with the abominable cover-ups **shock-open** Catholic world views? These unthinkable crimes have now been exposed at the end of the 20th century and are being continually unmasked in the 21st. Would this great unmasking bring about the needed revolution? Would these terrible revelations that have shaken the faith of so many Catholic people be an awakening of a more profound Christian faith? Would it begin the needed renewal initiated by the unsuccessfully completed Vatican II? So far into the 21st century it still has not happened but there are some significant indications. We must always remember that the Lord's time is not ours).*

After seven weeks of Monday meetings Father Steven's group was disbanded. We both agreed that much had been learned but much learning still remained. Father Steve and I were grateful for the experience. We were even more aware of this great truth: **(*Logical intellectually and historically rooted explanations are woefully insufficient*** *in gaining understanding and most especially acceptance of the changes proposed by Vatican II.)*

There were other elements in this admittedly difficult process. Some elements were far more effective. Among these were the long established choices, decisions, commitments, and relationships. But most of all were the emotional factors that were so powerful. Few, if any, were in evidence during our discussions. The opening letter of the Austrian Bishops continued to resound in both our increasing understanding.

Beware, Holy Father, the hierarchy and many more of the clergy are not prepared to understand nor accept the proposed changes of Vatican II.

In our small group of thoughtful young priests we had met this prediction head-on. Were we engaged in pushing a giant stone up a mountain only to have it roll down so we had to go back and roll it up again in a process without end? Were we facing a *world view* too entrenched to ever change?

Chapter 6
More corruption within the clerical culture revealed.

It was not long after our study group had disbanded that I received a surprise call from a pastor in a very affluent section of the city. He introduced himself as a long ago graduate of the same University in Europe where I had studied for four years and been ordained. As current president of his ordination class he was planning a 25th anniversary get-together of the member priests including our own bishop. They came from diocese throughout the U. S. So Father Edwards, the pastor of St. Luke's parish invited me to dinner to ask for my ideas concerning this coming summer big event. The rectory was even more elegant than the rectory of my summer assignment. All dinnerware and beverage glasses were trimmed in gold. Father Edwards had hired a violinist to quietly play during the evening. Most surprising was that his assistant, a priest, only a few years older than I, was our *server*. Dressed in a butler-like uniform, he did not join us at dinner but quietly *waited table* as if accustomed to this role. Though astonished, I made no comment. Rather I listened to the proposals for a four day weekend of golfing and enjoyment at an exclusive club on a scenic lake. Special housing accommodations would all be provided at the golf club's own resort hotel. In addition, weather permitting, excursion for a day of touring would be offered. All of this was to be with luxurious luncheons and dinners at three of Adamsburgh's finest restaurants. It was clear that Father Edwards was going to present a most impressive experience for his fellow ordination classmates *the gents*. Of course, the bishop of our diocese, also, a class member, would be the guest of honor at the opening dinner. After all, he was the paying sponsor for it all.

> Wel oghte a prest ensample for to yive
> By his clennesse, how that his sheep shold lyve
> And leet his sheep encombred in the myre
> A shitten shepherde and a clene sheep.

(Well ought a priest example to give. By his cleanliness how his sheep should live. And not leave his sheep encumbered in the filth. A shitten shepherd and a clean sheep.)

Canterbury Tales General Prologue II

I thanked the pastor, Father Edwards, for his hospitality and politely left St. Luke's rectory. I was deeply scandalized by the luxurious materialistic sense of entitlement I had just witnessed.

> *(The roots of his depravity would take many years to be unmasked. So it is by their fruits you shall know them.)*

But at the time I knew nothing. At least, I thought I had not revealed my true impressions. I was badly mistaken. Father Edwards was suspicious of me from that day. It was not what I said, but what I did not say. The negative element in my conversations had betrayed my real feelings. However it was not only the lavish life style that this priest was hiding behind.

> *(It still came as a chock to learn more than thirty years later when his victims exposed their sexual abuse at the hands of this deceased pedophile. His former altar boys, now in later life were finally making public the trauma that for so many years had overshadowed their lives Who of us newly ordained*

Chapter 6

priests in the early 1960's could have possibly believed these horrors? It was then secretly covered up by all those in authority. And what can be said about those who knew about these crimes but did nothing not even to help the victims? He who is silent consents!)

The second telephone call I had received provided an opportunity for another encounter with the cancerous clerical culture. It was from the executive of a psychiatric institution. The facility was located on a private road in a secluded section of Adamsburgh. The director asked for a meeting with me the following week. He related that he needed assistance with some of his priest-patients seeking understanding of Vatican II's proposals that might concern them. Through some members of his board of directors

He had learned I might be just the priest to help. I agreed to meet with him at a time of mutual convenience. And so began my introduction to a new world of scandal cover-up. The director explained that the institution had several priests in its care needing psychiatric treatment. They were from dioceses throughout the United States. At that time it was the strong belief that a priest's sexual deviant behaviors could be **addressed and perhaps cured.** He also emphasized that I would **not** be informed details of any of these **aberrations** that resulted in the placement of these priests at the institute. Nor should I permit any of these priests to reveal the reasons for their therapy. Hopefully, the outcome of this care would enable them to return to normal priestly life in the distant future. My role was to periodically meet with each priest. We might then have an informal one-on- one conversation about the renewals proposed by Vatican II. I had published a well received popular article and had impressed several members of the institution's board. Also they were impressed by my sermons at St. Hilary. The director now firmly believed I was ideally suited for this proposed project. At the time, I viewed this as opportunity to perhaps help fellow priests. With a few questions regarding locations, sessions, structures time restrictions, etc. I accepted the proposal on a prescribed trial period of three months. My class schedule at the college and my duties at St. Hilary on Thursday afternoons would accommodate this well. This also met the institution's schedules. Each priest was driven from the institute to St. Hilary for the first of these Thursday meetings. Our one hour sessions were held separately at 1, 2 or 3p.m. Rather than have these conversations in the stark too public first floor offices, I invited each priest up to my small living room on the third floor. This kindness and privacy was well noted. It seemed to relax them. I thought that after all they *were* fellow priests. By agreement with the director our meetings were limited to exactly one hour. After brief introductions, I began our conversations with information about Vatican II. The concerns presented by the recent study group at the College provided a workable framework. The second half hour was set aside for questions. This structure seemed to please each priest. But by the third sessions the questions were becoming more personal in nature. Each participant wanted to address specifically the problem that had brought him to the institute. The focus turned to measures Vatican II could take to ameliorate their situation as priests. Because of my open approach to their dignity they wondered if similar attitudes might be part of the changes in this renewal. I emphasized that I was engaged in this project *only* to explain the content of the proposals *now* being considered by Vatican II. I had no competency to answer their specific questions.

Because of the preoccupation of each participant with his own issues as well as the absence of questions and comments indicating near complete indifference to the issues of Vatican II led me to an uncomfortable suspicion. Was it that these priests considered participation in this learning project merely a method of establishing their eligibility to achieve early release from the institute? The director and I had assumed that their goal was greater understanding and eventual acceptance of Vatican II. But was theirs a practical goal quite different? It was time to bring this issue to the institute's director's board. Clearly we had reached an impasse. The director and I agreed that our noble well intentioned project had to be ended. Perhaps some benefit had been achieved. We certainly had tried. Like so many experiences since returning from Europe, I seemed to have benefited most of all.

It was only several years later I learned what the director had known. I now understood why he so quickly agreed to terminate the Vatican II education project with those priests. These men were expert deceivers who had masked their sexual assault on innocent children for years. Their bishops had sent them to the institute as a last resort hoping that psychiatric therapy might *cure* them. **I began to understand it never would**. The director was very wise in not revealing their vicious crimes to me. Knowing these facts, even given my naïve immaturity, I would have realized their situations were well beyond my inadequate capabilities.

Chapter 7
The joys and challenges of the learning process.

I no longer had the distraction of the institute's education project. The classes at the college would now receive greater attention. My courses were divided into two sections the first three days of the week. The morning class was composed entirely of first year nursing students. There were twenty two students. Half of these young women were novices in the religious order that served the Catholic hospital. The others were not. The afternoon class was entirely a combination of three different teaching religious communities. Some of these were novices, but most were young professed nuns completing their college degrees. This larger class had thirty five students. The morning section was the class in moral principles in the medical world. The afternoon section was entitled moral principles forming a Catholic education. Fortunately I had available bound volumes of notes and lectures from my studies in Europe together with access to copy machines at the college. The students were mature and very attentive. I employed a Socratic methodology using as little lecturing as possible. The renewal in the Church and the issues Vatican II was considering were of immense interest. So my study group labors had well prepared me to begin these courses with the challenges I faced.

Like the recently ordained priests of Father Steven's study group these young students were inquisitive enthusiastic learners. But also like that group was the *world-view* they brought with them. They were totally unprepared to understand and accept the **world view** I was about to present to them. I was ready. **But some were not.**

(As I look back over more than a half century since my teaching time at St. Thomas Aquinas College, the experience was mostly joyful and personally rewarding. Again, I helped most of the students to see the world around them in a much more positive light.)

For some few sisters the new way of re-examining their long cherished beliefs, myths and prejudices was just too much to accept. A few complained to their superiors within their community. The complaint reached Monsignor Alfred Bolger, the supervisor of religious orders of women within the diocese. He called me into his chancery office one afternoon to reprimand me for using a ***shocking*** word during one of my classes. I had referred to some fundamentalist type preachers as ***jackasses***. He said "This **horrific language** must never be used among these sensitive nuns. They are not strong enough for such language. ***After all, they are only women.***" I did not know how to respond. So I quietly thanked him for his advice. With a hardly concealed sneer, he dismissed me with a nod to the door.

(I discovered forty years later that this official member of the bishop's inner circle, a transplant from a far distant diocese, had been finally exposed as a serial pedophile. As usual it had been covered-up. He had been on loan from that diocese. Long deceased he had escaped this world's punishment for his abominable criminal behavior. But his victims would never be able to escape the impact of what he had done to them.)

Far more positively, I have lately discovered that some in those classes went on to become superiors of their religious communities. Others had gone on to chief positions in the medical profession. Hopefully

Chapter 7

the lessons of those classes were not forgotten. A few did write that they would never forget what they had learned.)

During my time at St. Hilary my duties continued to augment my reputation as an ***unusual*** priest. The Saturday confessional's lines and crowded 11a.m. Sunday sermons were attracting attention throughout the greater Adamsburgh area. This increased the number of assignments from the bishop's office to explain the renewal proposals of Vatican II. The requests were from area colleges and churches both Catholic and non-Catholic. There even were invitations from Synagogues from which no Catholic priest had ever been invited. My friend Father Steven, the University chaplain, was an advocate of some of these. But I learned that the main source was an advisor to the bishop himself. This priest had been one of my high school instructors many years past. With gratitude, I contacted him. This revitalized a friendship that continued for many years. Importantly, since the invitations were coming directly from the bishop, Father Vittor had no veto power over them. He perceived them to be a further imposition on my time away from St. Hilary. It certainly did not improve my relationship with him. In fact it became worse. But there were other much more serious reasons.

Through trusted anonymous sources I learned of a special association of senior citizens long ago established by Father Vittor when he was pastor of St. Theresa's parish. This *club* was a social and political voting organization. Its purpose was to influence the mayoral elections. With his leadership, it met for lunch once per month. At this meeting dues of $10 per person were collected ostensibly for the luncheon. In reality the luncheon was donated. The fee went to Father Vittor's personal finances. Among political matters he advised the club members as to the mayoral candidate for whom they should cast their vote. Possessing a unified voting block of more than 50 senior citizens gave Father Vittor significant political power. He used it. His move to St.

Hilary had continued this lucrative arrangement. The club had even grown as many seniors believed their former pastor had influenced the construction of the new affordable housing complex. No question was ever asked concerning the $10 monthly membership fee. It totaled at least $500 per luncheon. Over many years it was a very substantial sum. No record was ever made public. The two senior curates only speculated. One time they even dared to share their suspicions with me. But I do not believe the pastor's evident dislike of his *useless assistant* had anything to do with financial matters. The continued deterioration in our relationship was not because of my teaching assignments and the other non parish related activities all beyond his control. But it was the major devastating factor that struck him personally.

After spending more than a year at St. Hilary the *different priest* had a reputation as being a priest to consult who really listened with empathy and compassion. So it was not surprising that a young nun who was one of the teachers at the school came to speak to me privately in the first floor office of the rectory.

The young nun was choking back her tears. Her story was indeed tragic. She was being sexually assaulted by a priest. **He was her pastor**, Father Vittor. This crime had been going on for many weeks. She had begged him to stop. Instead he threatened to blame *her* for soliciting *him*. He had continued his assaults in her private hospital room during her recent visit there for minor surgery. His treachery knew no bounds.

She asked for my help to force him to stop. At this point she broke down tearfully saying, "I feel so guilty. Can you do anything? You are the only one I have told." She whispered this through her tears. I attempted to convince her that she had no guilt. I promised to do my very best to end this abuse without involving her in the scandal.

Chapter 7

Comforted and somewhat relieved she left to return to the nearby convent.

The next morning, **I made a colossal mistake**. Very stupidly I naively attempted to appeal to a fellow priest by **confronting him** with the harm he was doing. I asked him to end his sinful behavior. Unsurprisingly, he furiously told me to mind my own business. Then in anger he concluded with the statement, 'How dare y*ou* accuse **me**?" Knowing that I had acted with complete foolishness, I magnified my mistake, threatening to expose his criminality to the bishop. I had literally put my head into the mouth of a tiger. Then I asked the tiger not to bite it off. It took only two more weeks for the decapitation to take place.

It was a bright sunny Sunday afternoon in mid August. I had been on duty for the last two weeks. It was Andy's week on duty. He asked me to take any baptism candidates that might arrive. He planned to visit his ill brother. He promised to return by 2:15p.m. Andy had given Lucy his telephone number in case he might be delayed. That afternoon there were no candidates for baptism. Changed into my professional attire, I was leaving to attend my mother's 65th birthday party at my home many miles away. As I walked to my car in the rectory's garage, I passed the vault door unusually open. Then I heard the pastor shout out in anger "Where are *you* going?" Since I had taken the baptismal time he likely thought that I was on duty. I quickly explained that I had taken Andy's place as a favor. This was *his* week on duty. Moreover he had promised to return in a few moments after his quick visit to his ill brother. Continuing to raise his voice the angry pastor shouted, "**No he is not!** *You* **are on duty for the rest of the summer!**" Shocked, I told him that he was mistaken. I was leaving to attend my mother's birthday party. His response was: "**I order you remain here!**" At this point, I lost my temper. We engaged in a vehement shouting match ending in my telling him exactly what I thought of him. Getting into my car, I drove away leaving him standing there in a terrible rage.

The next morning, I received an urgent summons from my friend and advocate the bishop's closest advisor. The message was disturbing. I was to come to his office in the chancery as soon as possible. I had the sense that something serious had happened. At 10 a.m. I entered the chancery office expecting the worst. Father Russell, mow Monsignor Russell, welcomed me with a handshake but a sad expression. He began by telling me that my pastor had rushed in yesterday to speak with the bishop. His version of what had happened between the two of us had greatly upset the bishop. You see, Msgr. Russell explained, the bishop was about to assign you as the Catholic chaplain of Adamsburgh University. I was to replace Steven Harrison who had strongly recommended me. Steven was moving to the chancery as new Diocesan Director of Catholic Education. After Father Vittor's strong complaint, the bishop had reconsidered appointing me as University Catholic Chaplain. My friend advocate and former high school teacher asked if he might help me in any way. Astonished and devastated by what I had just learned I told him there was far more to Father Vittor's anger with me than merely my non parish assignments. True, he believed these assignments coming from the chancery took me away from my duties as his **useless junior assistant.**

I then described in detail the confrontation with him regarding his sexual molestations and assaults on the young teacher at St. Hilary grammar school. I further related the pastor's promise to get rid of me for these accusations. Finally I described his reaction to my rejected **fellow priest pleas** to discontinue his sinful behavior.

It was now Msgr. Russell who was shocked. With great understanding, he took my hand saying, "Joe this certainly changes things a great deal. Do not worry. I will speak to the bishop. We will take

Chapter 7

care of this right away."Greatly relieved but fearing what might happen I returned to my rooms at St. Hilary. By Monday morning John and Andy had already learned of the Sunday afternoon confrontation, their concern was that the pastor's frightful mood would somehow impact *their lives*. Their advice was to keep a low profile and remain on duty the entire week. The *boss* was to leave for his vacation on Saturday. Perhaps when he returned the storm might pass. Knowing what I knew, I did not believe a word of it. But I accepted their advice to remain silent. I did not have long to wait. The letter from the chancery office arrived special delivery on Tuesday morning the very next day.

My friend and advocate, Monsignor Russell had truly ***taken care of it***. I was to continue in my faculty position at St. Thomas Aquinas College. In addition I was to remain as the bishop's spokesperson on Vatican II proposals in all future assignments especially with the non-Catholic Christian and Jewish communities. Lastly, I was to report to Monsignor George Bannon the pastor of St. Marc's nearby church on this Friday afternoon. The letter did not mention that St. Marc's parish was the largest and most prestigious parish in the diocese. Among its many parishioners were members of both medical and educational leaders in the community. In addition residing there were the most powerful corporation executives in the diocese. As I related my news to John and Andy, I learned that Father Anton Vittor was not leaving for vacation. He was now summoned to meet with the bishop in private. He had already been told of my new appointment to St. Marc's and the announcement that I was not to be replaced by a third assistant. It was strongly suggested by the senior assistants that I should leave St. Hilary as quickly as possible.

To prepare for my new assignment on Friday my very first call was to Monsignor Russell to thank him for his intercession. Naturally he would only tell me he hoped I would enjoy the new appointment. The next few days were spent alerting my many friends at St. Hilary of my new appointment as well as the new ways I might be reached. I had no contact at all with Father Vittor. It seemed best that way. As time elapsed, I never heard from him nor did I ever see him again. *(He died long ago.)*

Chapter 8
The decade of the 1960's continued.

(I believe there is no better description of my most significant time as an active priest in the decade of the 1960's than Charles Dickens opening paragraph in his masterful work **A Tale of Two Cities***. I quote it here in its entirety.)*

"It was the best of times, it was the worst of times, it was the age of wisdom, it was the age of foolishness, it was the epoch of believers, it was the epoch of incredulity, it was the season of Light, it was the season of Darkness, it was the spring of hope, it was the winter of despair, we had everything before us, we had nothing before us, we were all going direct to Heaven, we were all going direct the other way- in short, the period was so far like the present period that some of its noisiest authorities insisted on its being received, for good or for evil, in the superlative degree of comparison only."

The cultural upheaval of the 1960's was not only bringing about a renewal for the entire Catholic Church but the winds of change were everywhere. Slowly taking hold in the United States, Vatican II was seemingly a spring of hope. Then the death of Pope John XXIII surprised and dampened that hope. The winter clouds of rejection the Austrian Bishops had forewarned were gathering quickly. As soon as the amazing visionary Pope John XXIII had died a new Pope was elected taking the name Paul VI. Before his election he had been Cardinal Giovanni Battista Montini the Archbishop of Milan and Secretary of State for Pope Pius XII, Powerful members of the Curia, the Catholic Church's bureaucracy, a significant part of the papal inner circle, were very conservative **opponents** of Pope John XXIII's progressive policies. Above all it was his establishment of Vatican II they resented. These priests, bishops and some cardinals were active practitioners within the **corrupt clerical culture**. They had begun to plot their course of action even before the surprising death of Pope John XXIII. His death had happened shortly after the first full year of Vatican II. This left the Council remaining decidedly incomplete. These were the forces that had waited until the attempts of renewal could quickly be put to rest. They were led by none other than the pope's Secretary of State Cardinal Alfredo Ottoviani. He was the most radically conservative member of the Roman Curia. Great to their surprise and dismay was the decision of the reserved new Pope Paul VI to continue the Ecumenical Council, Vatican II. They would have to continue to exercise patience and rely on their powerful Cardinal Otaviani to quietly and effectively to lead them. **This he did masterfully.**

As instructed, I reported to St, Marc's rectory that Friday afternoon at 1 p.m. sharp. My reputation as a ***maverick liberal*** with all the negative connotations it often entails preceded me as sure as night follows day. Before meeting with the priests with whom I would be living I had done the best research I could. I discovered that the pastor, Monsignor George Bannon, had been a chaplain in the U.S. Air Force during WW II. His duties had kept him safe in the United States during the entire war. He had been rewarded for his military service by his appointment as the pastor of St. Marc's parish. Celebrated throughout the diocese, St. Mark's was definitely the largest and most prestigious parish. Indeed, it was the ***plum*** appointment. Its parishioners were numbered among the most highly educated in any diocese. It was

Chapter 8

home to the wealthiest Catholics in the entire state. In fact among its Catholics were the Bishop of the Diocese and the Governor of the State. In addition resided chief executives of some major corporations. Besides this, a large number of its very active and generous parishioners were members of the medical and academic communities.

Not immediately on the day of his appointment but soon after it, he was named a domestic prelate. ***Monsignor* Bannon** was the ideal image for his new role. If a motion picture casting professional were in search of a Gregory Peck look-a-like he would look no further than Monsignor George Bannon. He was very tall and exceptionally well groomed with wavy gray hair. One would find him always attired in a black red buttoned cassock, a red silk sash and a red silk lined and red trimmed small cape. His appearance was the ideal image immediately ready for television. However, my research was superficial. Beneath the image was a greedy, autocratic narcissist. The first indication of the actual Msgr. Bannon was before dinner Friday afternoon. Without pretending cordiality were his opening words, "I hope you are not going to cause any trouble while you are here. I am not pleased **that you** have been assigned to this parish. **Your *maverick reputations* precede you.** The other priests will show you to your quarters and explain operations here at St. Marc's. This is all I have to say to you for now." With that I was dismissed with a nod at the door. I did not know then what was to be a series of most unpleasant experiences for me and everyone else present as he presided at the evening dinner table.

Quickly that afternoon the other two assistants met with me individually. Each met in his own suit of rooms. The senior assistant, Father Peter Burkman, was exceedingly formal. Like the pastor he was very concerned that I would be an upsetting factor in the major task of keeping the *boss* always contented. This was something very important to Peter Burkmn. He enjoyed an extraordinary amount of **free time** as senior assistant as well as the Catholic chaplain of the Boy Scouts in the diocese. His junior, Father Tom Ford was daily occupied as the principal of St. Marc's Catholic grammar school. It was located on the extensive grounds of the church. Father Tom was dedicated to the children of the school. He kept contact with them even as they moved on in their education. The children and their parents were very fond of Father Tom. He was truly one of the good shepherds deeply caring for his flock. His welcome was warm and cheerful. Very soon he and I became the best of friends. We both resided on the top floor of the very large red brick rectory. Each priest had a suite of three rooms consisting of a bath room, a bed room and a living room. Tom and one of the resident priests, the elderly Charles Forester director of the Catholic Library, had much larger living rooms than I. All three of us were on this top floor. Peter Burkman, Bob Saunders, assistant director of the diocesan news paper and the Monsignor were on the second floor in the three largest suites. Nevertheless my smaller quarters were very adequate. I did not consider this as an indication of my designation as the **maverick curate.** That however was made clear the first evening at that unforgettable dinner. Monsignor Bannon in full red rimmed attire presided at the head of a long oak table. On his left were seated the guest residents. On his right were his two senior assistants. At the far end facing him was my position.

There was little doubt who commanded the conversation. Focusing his attention directly on me, he began asking what I thought of a statement he had heard that afternoon on his favorite radio station. This always presented far-right conservative Catholic opinions. That afternoon the commentator had accused the Austrian bishops of ridiculing the American bishops for being unprepared to accept the pronouncements of the Ecumenical Council. "As a great *expert* on Vatican II, what *Father* do you think of **that**?" began the *boss*. The sarcasm in the question's tone was dripping with venom. An uncomfortable silence permeated the atmosphere. Sensing an impending confrontation, I quietly replied that perhaps the commentator had misunderstood the

Chapter 8

Austrian Bishops letter to Pope John XXIII. The letter was **not** an accusation directed to any nation's hierarchy. It was merely a warning regarding the current lack of preparation within the entire clerical caste leadership of the Church itself. This letter was rather a call to do more preparation **by the Council.** It simply urged them to **prepare** the entire clergy for what its proposals might be suggesting. My somewhat complex answer seemed to defuse the situation for the moment. But everyone present realized that this was not the end but only the beginning. **They were not wrong.** The grand Inquisition was just adjusting its sights

This targeted *assault* continued. Each evening during dinner I quickly learned that **any** answer was never going to be acceptable or even expected. A clear rebuttal would only produce an even more sarcastic response. This inevitably led to more uncomfortable silence throughout the remainder of dinner. Clearly the best response was to be silent and not respond. This was1 quickly impressed upon me by the other priests present. They also learned to distract the Monsignor with non-controversial matters. It was necessary for me to accept the ancient wisdom already noted: **"Anyone who is silent, appears to consent".** In any event, after several weeks, Monsignor Bannon himself grew weary of his game. A new and even much greater concern had upset him. His parish was about to be divided. The news had come from the chancery office. A new parish was to be established. It was to consist of the western 25% of St. Marc's parish. The letter did not mention that this 25% of St. Marc's was the home of the wealthiest and most influential families in all Adamsburgh. As noted, here resided the majority of the corporate executives the college and university leaders, the large group of medical professionals as well as the most successful small business owners. Among these residents a significant number were current active parishioners as well as generous contributors to St, Marc's. This last factor was of the greatest concern to Msgr. George Bannon. For the next two weeks he spent his time with his unmarried brother and sister at their luxurious home far from the city. He told Father Burkman that he decided to go on a family trip. So except for his most trusted assistant Peter Burkman and his secretary Marianne Murray he was on vacation from St. Marc's for two weeks. But awful news continued to await him.

The first change concerned the population of the rectory. Robert (Bob) Saunders the assistant editor of the diocesan newspaper was moving to quarters in the chancery. He would now be living in the same residence as the editor. In his place until his new rectory could be established would be Father John McNamara the newly appointed pastor of the new parish Church of Christ the King. This new division of St. Marc's was the stunning blow from which Msgr. Bannon's all consuming greed would never recover.

Father "Mac" was the well celebrated principal of East Catholic High School This was going to be the first time ever for him as a pastor of a parish. During the past two decades he had guided E.C.H. in both academics and athletics to its position as one of the top ten high schools in the entire North Eastern U.S. In honoring Fr. Mac and his great achievements the Bishop of Adamsburgh had appointed him to be pastor of the newest **plum** parish community in the diocese. Then the chancery team made a terrible mistake. It appeared to the bishop's office that placing Father McNamara in residence among his fellow priests at St. Marc's rectory would give him a smooth transition allowing him to become acquainted with some of his new flock and the environment of his new parish. It did not turn out to be as beneficial as believed. No one had conceived the untenable position that would face John McNamara living in residence at St. Marc's rectory.

Monsignor George Bannon had returned two weeks ahead of the changes at the rectory. His so called vacation had not ameliorated his foul mood. If anything, it seemed to intensify it. To Tom and

Chapter 8

me his resentment was evident. It took only a few days after John McNamara arrived for this wise and gentle man to see through the faked politeness to the deep seated anger and resentment. The dinner hour was a continuous full blown **sarcastic inquisition.** This time I was not the target. John McNamara was far wiser than I had been. Within a very short time Father "Mac" had rented a large single family house in a section of his new parish. He also had leased large space in a middle school gymnasium near the new parish area in which to hold Sunday Mass for his new flock. The bishop's office, well aware of the reasons for the move, had provided the needed funds. Perhaps no other behavior of Msgr. Bannon was more indicative of his greed and betrayal of any understanding of Christ-like behavior to a fellow priest than his treatment of Father Mac.

For if gold ruste, what shall iron do…For if a preest be foul, on whom we truste,

No wonder is a lewed man to ruste, And shame it is, if a preest take keep. A shitten shepherde and a clene sheep.

(For if gold rust, what shall iron do? For if a priest be foul in whom we trust,
No wonder is a poor layman to sin terribly.
And shame it is if a priest betray his promises A shitten shepherd and clean sheep.)

As the weeks past, Msgr. Bannon continued to brood but nevertheless continue his autocratic and narcissistic ways. This included his tendencies to forget practical matters, such as the names of his parishioners. This happened as he was trying to impress them with his apparent empathy as when he was at the church's front door greeting the coffin of a deceased spouse of a wealthy parishioner, He would have turned to Tom or me as he walked down the aisle asking the name of the widow or widower before using their first names pouring out his sympathy with hypocritical remorse. He only officiated at the funerals of the wealthy.

In addition, he often omitted critical portions of the Mass he was celebrating. When confronted, he denied this vehemently. He had adopted a behavior long informed by a profound theological error. This involved the ignorant materialistic belief that the breath of the celebrant was somehow more effective when whispered as loudly as possible.

(This fallacy originates in medieval times when the Mass was celebrated behind a large wooden wall. This was done to keep the sinful peasants away from the sanctuary reserved for the exclusive noblemen and their equally exclusive clergy. Thus the poor uneducated layman, the lewed man of Chaucer's epic, could only hear what sounded like **Hocus Pocus***. This became a common expression for anything mysterious and incapable of being understood.)*

The central words of the Eucharist celebration: "For this is my body" spoken in Latin, **Hoc Est enim Corpus Meum** has continued this verbal anomaly to this day. So it was that Msgr. Bannon took great satisfaction in whispering as loudly as possible the key words of the Eucharist *(though now in English)*.Importantly he neglected to emphasize the highly significant phrase which follows-**Do this in Memory of Me.** The depth of theological and historical ignorance that he embraced completely escaped him.

What he could not deny was several times backing his car out of the garage while destroying the close doors. The evidence for this was indisputable. Even more disastrous was the use of parish funds to erect a tall metal spire on top the tower at the front of the church building. This was revealed only when this fifty thousand dollar ***dunce cap*** was

Chapter 8

lowered into place by a helicopter as a large group of workmen installed it. This object imitated the spires on towers of some European church buildings No one knew anything of this project or its cost but Msgr. Bannon and his brother and sister. They had seen such additions on their many excursions to Europe. With no consultation the decision was exclusively theirs. Nevertheless Marianne, the know-it-all parish secretary, soon discovered all the details.

Through her private network she told all. The major secret she shared only with a few including Peter Burkman was the more than $25,000 per year Christmas collections designated for the **priests** of the parish. This was the content of the two large black satchels carried away by the brother and sister on the next day after Christmas. Here was the real reason they always came for dinner on Christmas Eve without fail. They departed quietly on the afternoon of Christmas day only after all the priests had left to be with family and friends. But Marianne always saw the two leave. She also shared with Father Burkman photos of the Bannon's **manor estate** on a large lake in an exclusive part of the state. This was an area where only the wealthiest of the wealthy resided. Was it any wonder that Peter Burkman sometimes, but rarely, revealed his bitterness to Tom as he distributed the $300 gift. This supposed Christmas gift for each priest of the parish came in the form of a check signed by Msgr. Bannon himself. It was drawn on his personal checking account to demonstrate his claimed benevolence to his assistants. He revealed to Marianne that it truly upset him deeply to sign **my** check.

In that final year that St. Marc's parish was partitioned, the Christmas collection for the priests of the parish was greatly impacted. Nonetheless many of the wealthy parishioners still made a secret financial Christmas gift to the priests of their former parish. The brother and sister still arrived for Christmas-eve dinner and departed the following afternoon with their two heavy black satchels in tow. In it were the secret gifts for the priests of the parish. Marianne reported to Peter Burkman that the collection was down but only by a few thousand dollars. That week Msgr. Bannon declared that the Christmas gift for the priests would be just $250 each. The check continued to be signed by Msgr. Bannon himself. We were not surprised at all. **His narcissism and greed knew no limitations**.

For if gold rust, what shall iron do……For if a preest be foul…A shitten shepherde…

Chapter 9
My last years at St. Marc's. The decade of the 60's closes.

My final years at St. Marc's parish were truly the best and the worst of times Hearing confessions continued to be the greatest source of my increased understanding of the overwhelming burdens the Catholic people were suffering. I did my very best to provide helpful counsel in a context which was impersonal, anonymous and highly restrictive. I became increasingly aware that my efforts were so inadequate. However the long lines continued to grow longer each Saturday. Maybe my compassion and listening skills were communicated by my few words. Nevertheless, I could not shake the sense that I was not really impacting the intense guilt I encountered. This was especially true of the women and men whose youth was identified by the sound of their voices. These were nearly breaking as they recounted being **sexually abused by priests they had trusted**. Even if they had identified these priests, which they never did, the seal of the confessional bound me solemnly. I always believed and still do that it was far greater than any attorney-client privilege. My brief experience at the institute in no way had prepared me for what I learned in my few years in the confessional. And I could do nothing but curse the darkness and my often ineffectual silence which I knew often seemed to give consent.

On rare occasions, Msgr. Bannon and Peter Burkman would enter the church having notice the high volume of cars outside. They would then each erect a portable kneeling device equipped with a screen. Placed in the far front behind the marble communion railing, they would in loud voices announce:"There is more than one priest hearing confessions!" They sat behind the makeshift screen with no anonymity or privacy provided. Should they have wondered why so many people headed for the exits rather than heed their loud angry announcement?

It is important to note that St. Marc's church building had a lower as well as an upper main area which could accommodate the celebration of two Masses simultaneously. While almost never used in the past. Sunday's 11 o'clock Mass was attracting such a large attendance necessitating the use of both levels. Because I always celebrated the 11 o'clock Mass in the upper level, a curious population adjustment would occur. It was doubtlessly the content of my sermons focusing on changes proposed by Vatican II. Beside that there was also the division between the more conservative traditionally minded parishioners and the more liberal and more progressive minded. As I appeared in the upper level several minutes before Mass was to begin, a significant number of people would leave to go downstairs to attend Mass celebrated by Peter Burkman. An equal number from the lower level would ascend to the upper level. This curious migration became a common Sunday morning occurrence. Many parishioners found it amusing.

The stark division among traditional and progressive Catholic attitudes was impressed upon me quite forcefully at a local school board meeting. My good friend Dr. Robert Shaw was chairman of the school board as well as the academic dean of the University where I was teaching. He and his wife were very active parishioners of St. Marc's. Inviting me to that meeting, he promised me it was to be a super charged event. Your presence would be greatly appreciated was added to his invitation. **He was not mistaken.** I arrived a few minutes late, delayed by a demand conference at the rectory called by Msgr.

Bannon to announce his plans to be taking more personal time at his so called vacation home. He claimed that his need for more rest and quiet was at the recommendation of his doctor.

The delay proved to be most unfortunate. This hearing's purpose was to present plans to-school bus a small number of grammar school children from the inner city of Adamsburgh to be distributed equally to all the grammar schools of West Adamsburgh. This would include The Hebrew Grammar School and St. Marc's Catholic Grammar School the only two non-public schools in town. I entered the large auditorium as the audience was just completing vilifying Rabbi Goldman. I later learned he had been explaining the benefits for *all the children* this proposal would provide. The anti–Semite and racist shouts had hardly subsided when Dr. Shaw recognized my raised hand. I was asking to be heard. He and I had spent time talking about this proposal to bring inner-city children, all from the African-American and Hispanic-American population, into the town's schools. So I was prepared to offer my views. What I was not prepared for was that the majority of angry faces in the audience were faces of parishioners of St. Marc's parish. Like Rabbi Goldman my explanations emphasizing a moral responsibility as a people of faith was met with insults, racist slurs and vicious calls to "*shut up liberal* and *sit down N...lover*". In shame and shock I did. At that moment my reliance on my shield of protection as a Catholic priest confronting racism provoked angry sun-shine Catholics was manifestly nonexistent. Standing in the pulpit at the eleven o'clock Mass the following Sunday, I noted that the faces I had seen at that school board meeting were not to be seen before me. No doubt they were at the Mass being celebrated in the lower level by Peter Burkman. It was no surprise that this celebration always ended earlier than the upper level one. Father Burkman's brief non provoking sermons and rapid fire recitation of the prayers of the Mass were well appreciated by this congregation.

(There was never any church renewal or anti-war nonsense to be heard down here was the often repeated comment by the lower level attendees as Maryann was sure to tell me.)

Events related to opportunities to implement some of the new changes permitted and advocated by Vatican II continued to take place. The first I implemented in concert with someone who was becoming a close friend also a fellow instructor at the University. He was Reverend Jason Webb, the senior minister of the Congregational Church of West Adamsburgh. A young woman, a member of his congregation, was engaged to be married to a young man who just happened to be a parishioner of St. Marc's. According to a new prescription of Vatican II, the Catholic Bishop could grant his permission for the marriage to be celebrated in the Christian church of the non-Catholic member with both priest and minister jointly officiating. This celebration had never taken place in the diocese of Adamsburgh or in any other known dioceses in the eastern U.S. Therefore when Adamsburgh's Catholic Bishop's gave consent this ground-breaking event took place. Before a large audience of families and friends of both bride and groom, Jason and I concelebrated this marriage of a Protestant bride and a Catholic groom in the First Congregational Church of West Adamsburgh. It was famously the first of its kind. Not many days later, my friend and advocate at the chancery called to ask why I had sent the minister to ask the bishop to grant this permission and not come myself. I told him that I thought having the minister do the asking was just good politics. I could hear him quietly laughing at the other end of the phone. He knew I was learning very well.

The success of the concelebrated marriage ceremony inspired me to undertake a further implementation of a change urged by the Ecumenical Council. This concerned the administration of the sacrament known traditionally as the last rites. Vatican II had gently suggested that a more accurate understanding of this sacrament of the

Chapter 9

anointing of the body would assist in aiding the person to be restored to health. Thus it was truly the *Sacrament of the Sick*. Because I was so often away on speaking assignments, it seemed appropriate to Msgr. Bannon that I be made the parish chaplain to the two large nursing homes located within the parish. Actually this meant that all calls to anoint some patient at one of these homes seen as near death or already just died should now be given to the designated chaplain. Since these calls were most often in the middle of the night, this assignment was truly not an honor but seen as a punishment. Inspired and reinforced by valid theological correctness and changes of Vatican II, I instituted with no objection from anyone *a new practice* for the administration of this sacrament. With the cooperation of the administrations of both nursing homes I proposed to celebrate an afternoon Mass once per month in each location's large dining hall. As part of this Eucharist celebration I would preach a brief sermon, distribute communion and anoint the head and feet of each Catholic patient. This monthly celebration not only was a meaningful benefit to all the residents but an additional positive feature of each facility. Yes I did not doubt that some few of the residents anointed with the *Sacrament of the Sick* were not Catholic, but I was certain that the *Good Shepherd* did not mind so nether should I. It did put an end to the middle of the night calls to anoint the dead or nearly dead. But much more than this, it was a tiny step on the journey to *renewal in the Church* so hoped for by Pope John XXIII when he established the Ecumenical Council now forever to be known as Vatican II.

Msgr. Bannon's weekly absence Sunday noon until his return at noon on the following Friday was a welcome respite to all the resident priests at St. Marc's rectory. His brother had assumed the role of chauffeur driving his increasingly forgetful older brother to and from the manor house. Leaving on Sunday and arriving on Friday for the traditional two inch thick lamb chop dinner did not seem a burden to this younger sibling. This was the case although the round trip was nearly 60 miles. With his absence during my Sunday afternoon required presence, I had the opportunity to inaugurate another of Vatican II renewal practices. This concerned the important modification of the sacrament of Baptism. Since this was the entrance rite to the Christian Community it would be best symbolized by leading the person into the church building itself. So I proceeded to have the parents of the new born together with the sponsors and any relatives and friends meet me at the doors of the church building, (inside if the weather was inclement). Then in a very brief explanation of the ceremony we together engaged in a welcoming of the person, in most cases a recently born child, into the Christian Community *The Mystical Body of Christ.* Then with all present we proceeded to the baptismal font. This was in the small chapel near the sanctuary and altar of the church building. At this point, as the celebrant, I would distribute the ornate ritual book, the vial of anointing oil, the large Easter candle and any other instruments to aid in the pouring of the baptismal water. I sought to involve as many present as possible in the ceremony itself. I shall never forget a particular baptism in which the grandparents of the child were not Catholic but Jewish. Regardless, I asked their assistance in holding the ritual book and the Easter candle. This was the highest honor for all present. With tears in their eyes and great joy on their faces they both agreed. It was an inspiration for everyone who had taken part in not the usual but exceedingly meaningful and unforgettable celebration. (***Where there are two or more gathered together in my name, I am there in their midst, said the Lord Jesus.***)

Nevertheless the most memorable moments of those Sunday afternoons were those seven events that were on a par with my emotional experience at the first Mass I celebrated at the Carmelite chapel in Dachau. Being the Sunday afternoon priest nearly always on duty I was called upon to follow two military officers in my own car bringing the very first announcement to the family. Their son or daughter had been killed in action in the Vietnam War. The officers asked that I go before them to the front door of the house. And so I always did.

When the door opened, the mother, father or both greeted me with a surprised look of joyful welcome. Then they saw the two officers, usually young Army or Marine Lieutenants, standing behind me. Immediately they knew what this meant. The mother with a cry of anguish collapsed at my feet. The father shaken with tears just grabbed my hands. There were no words. At this moment one of the officers began a sterile recitation describing the time and place of the incident, the military unit involved etc. This was followed by an expression of sorrow and regret by the President and the Secretary of Defense. With this formal conclusion the two offices saluted. They then turned and quickly left. We stood in silence for some time. The pain among us all was overwhelming. In one of the seven of these tragic events it was not parents who met us at the door but the eight month pregnant wife. Her husband of but two years had been a medical-evacuation helicopter pilot. I will never forget her cries of despair as she collapsed at my feet. These are the soul searing memories I will take from this time at St. Marc's. As I write about them now, I relive the sadness and shed tears of anguish all over again.

These events foreshadowed the escalating disruption that was griping our nation. Protests were erupting on many of our college campuses. The major newspapers and television news programs continued to report the rising death tolls of American troops and even the horrible devastation in North Vietnam especially to its civilian population. This included reports of scandalous massacres being committed by our South Vietnamese allies and even some committed by members of our own military. Rabbi Goldman of Beth Shalom Synagogue had sponsored a presentation by an Anglican bishop, an anti-war activist. The invitation had gone out to all religious leaders of Adamsburgh. The conference was to be held in the large auditorium of the Rabbi's

Synagogue. My friend and advocate at the chancery had urged me to attend. Sadly I was the <u>*only*</u> Catholic priest in attendance. The speaker delivered a powerful message. He urged those present to ***do their homework*** and become educated regarding the tragic realities of our nation's involvement in what he called an ***immoral conflict***. He cited an abundance of evidence to establish the factual basis of his positions. For me, his presentation was extraordinarily eye-opening. The concluding statement was a plea that we also become aware of our responsibility to educate our congregations. The question period that followed indicated that his presentation had met with a lukewarm response, even rejection. But not all of us were of that mind. My experiences delivering those messages of intense sorrow found fertile ground for his presentation. This resulted in ***doing my homework***. I engaged in extensive research investigating our American involvement in this **War in Vietnam.**

(Barbara W. Tuchman, the prize winning historian would later call this war a significant giant step in her book The March of Folly. Succeeding events and revelations have proved her analysis exceedingly accurate.)

In my Sunday sermons I began to describe those soul searing announcements that I had been involved in delivering. I also asked the unanswered questions regarding the fact that the men and women killed in action disproportionally were often mostly the poor members as well as a large numbers of the racial minorities in our society. **T*he last straw*** took place as I initiated a moment of silence at the end of each Sunday sermon to commemorate by naming those who had been killed in action the previous week. Letters of condemnation began to frequent my mail. (***Stop mixing religion in politic!***) (***Keep God out of politics!***) *(The utter insanity of these statements is beyond belief.)*

Chapter 9

There was a significant increase in the number of Sunday Mass-goers moving to the lower church at the beginning of the 11 o-clock Eucharistic celebration. The main upper level used to be the significant Mass of the week for nearly all parishioners but no longer. It was evident that the divisiveness between the traditional and progressive Catholics was increasing. This was not really upsetting Msgr. George Bannon. As long as this did not impact the collection it was of little concern to him.

But this did. One of the resident priests of St. Marc's rectory had been *disappeared without a trace or explanation*. Father Charles Forester, the elderly director of the Catholic Library had been called back by his bishop in a distant diocese of the country. There had always been an unspoken question about his mysterious appearance so far away from his home diocese. There was a mystery as to his loan status to the Adamsburgh diocese. Msgr. Bannon alone knew the details of this arrangement. But he never revealed them not even to his know-it-all secretary Marianne. Not even did he tell his trusted assistant Peter Burkman. It was only years later that the story emerged. It seemed that, like so many other pedophile priests, Father Forester had been granted refuge in a far away diocese. This was advocated by a friend in high places. Having served as a chaplain in the Air Force during World War II it seemed appropriate that a fellow Air Force chaplain, Msgr. George Bannon, would supervise this semi-retirement. There was supposed to be a twice yearly report about Father Forester filed with the chancery office by Msgr. Bannon. But there never was. It seemed his forgetfulness knew almost no bounds. Unfortunately for me, I was never part of his memory lapses.

It turned out that his **liberal trouble-making maverick assistant** was becoming ever more intolerable than he could accept. In August of what was to be my last weeks at St. Marc's was the surprise. A letter from a distant prestigious university arrived. My application for graduate student status with full scholarship was offered. I learned that my application was greatly enhanced by the letters of recommendation written by several nationally known influential parishioners of St. Marc's parish. With great joy I immediately accepted. My decision to end my position as a member of the Catholic clergy long pondered but gradually solidified as inevitable was firmly decided.

Contacting my friend and advocate at the chancery, Msgr. Russell, I sought an appointment with the bishop to officially resign. My meeting was arranged for the next morning. I knew this was not going to be an amiable confrontation. I was as prepared as could be. I had not seen my bishop in person for quite some time. He appeared tired and older than I recalled. I announced that my first reason to meet him was to thank him for the many opportunities to explain the proposals of the Ecumenical Council. In this opening meeting I noted that the prediction of the Austrian Bishops delegation was proving true. Indeed it had been clear that Protestant, Jewish and secular leaders to whom I spoke seemed more receptive to the Council's proposals of renewal than most of the Catholic clergy. It was now time for the heart of the matter. I announced my acceptance to advance my academic studies as well as my proposal to resign as a priest, a member of the Catholic clergy. "I will not give you permission to do either of these things!" was his stern and barely controlled angry statement. As gently as I could I replied that I had not come to ask his permission but to state my gratitude for his confidence and guidance. Besides I had come to say that my decisions were steadfast. He then said. "You will get no assistance from me or this diocese if you persist in this course of action. I am *very disappointed* in you." The expression on his face became one of deep sadness. He then motioned with is hand to the door dismissing me. Without another word I left quietly never to see him again. The chancery office remained silent. There were no explanations forthcoming. No announcements were published.

Chapter 9

(Years later, Tom told me that at the very time of my conversation with the bishop he was undergoing chemotherapy for fourth stage pancreatic cancer. He died within the year.)

The report of my meeting with the bishop already reached St. Marc's rectory before I had even returned that morning. Msgr. Bannon had given word to his two assistants that I was to leave immediately. He had already informed Marianne his trusted secretary that I had not resigned but had been fired and would soon likely be excommunicated in disgrace. He announced that there was to be no farewell party with a substantial monetary gift. This was usually given to priests leaving their position at St. Marc's. He told everyone who would listen that he would shed no tears for that **useless liberal maverick curate.**

Tom helped me pack my small belongings and leave that afternoon. In the next few days I contacted my large number of my friends among the parishioners. Many had already heard the rumors being spread by those who were glad I was leaving. The rumors however were being countered by a true accounting of my resignation and its reasons. Congratulations regarding my acceptance of a scholarship to graduate studies at one of the nation's prestigious universities came quickly. I believe Father Tom had a large role in setting the record straight. By early September I had become a new post graduate student and my new life was just beginning. My fond memories of the many friends, relationships and positive experiences at St. Marc's parish in Adamsburgh will remain with me always.

That connection process was aided immensely by my continuous deep friendship with Father Tom Ford. In fact it was his intercession with chancery that sped up the action by that very chancery office to obtain from Pope Paul VI that complicated document called a rescript. It was this that gave me permission to eventually marry and remain a validated Catholic. It was also through Tom's information network I soon learned that my friend Father Steve Harrison had left the chancery position and taken a new appointment to a position in a Canadian University. Some few years later he too resigned from the practicing priesthood. There was not too surprising news regarding Peter Burkman. Accusations had arisen regarding sexual assaults among the leadership of the Boy Scouts of the Adamsburgh diocese. Within the year of this scandal, Peter Burkman was unceremoniously appointed as pastor of a small rural parish in the farthest limits of the diocese. Several years later a new pastor was appointed to that parish and Peter Burkman was said to have been *early retired.* Tom could obtain no further information. The chancery office remained silent. No doubt the process of cover-up was still fully in force.

My astonishment was real when seven years after I had left St. Marc's, my best friend Tom had left to marry a woman he had met at a national conference of school principals. After a few short months they both moved to her home in a distant state. We continued to correspond and even visited as often as we could. Tom's network of classmates remained active. It informed him and thus me as well regarding the lack of new seminarians nationwide and the continuing resignations of young priests. But most of all was the increasing revelations of sexual abuse by priests, bishops and even cardinals not only in the United States but in foreign countries as well. **The Scandals in the Catholic Church** continued to be unmasked. Would they never end?

(The answer remains unanswered!)

Chapter 10
Concluding perspectives in the present time.

At the beginning of the 21st century all these stories have led up to the on-going *scandals*. This is the horrific *crisis* now facing the Catholic Church. **Catholic** means **universal**. These *scanda*ls are truly universal in scope. A *crisis* of this magnitude has caused its unspeakable horror not only in the American Catholic Community but in every Catholic Community in the world. Finally the *scandals* have unearthed this abominable clerical culture. It is this clerical culture's century's old elements that are the **true causes** of the **scandals** that are shaking the faith of so many. These *scandals* have threatened to destroy the stability of the Catholic Church as an institution itself. In his Christmas address of 2018, Pope Francis harshly spoke out against those priests who had violated children, young men and young women. This is what he said directly to them. *"Hand yourself over to human justice and prepare for divine justice."* He went on to condemn these priests and even some bishops angrily stating: *They perform abominable acts yet continue to exercise their ministry as if nothing had happened. They have no fear of God or his judgment but only of being found out and unmasked.* In conclusion Pope Francis added, *"With their boundless amiability, impeccable activity and angelic faces they shamelessly conceal a vicious wolf ready to devour innocent souls."* Sadly this horrible crime against innocent souls was not at first revealed by Pope Francis and his recent three predecessors. It was the result of the Boston Globe's earth shaking reports now more than 17 years ago. Those reports exposed the abuse of children in the

Boston archdiocese. These reporters were astounded to discover that there existed such a large numbers of priests involved. They were also horrified by the callous manner in which all the victims were treated. This included the near universal practice of cover-ups and denials by bishops. It became worse. Some of these predatory priests became bishops. Some were even rewarded with the rank of cardinal as members of the papal inner circle.

At last the law is catching up with this long history of abuses and cover-ups. These actions have taken far too long. Many predators have died. Some are hiding behind statutes of limitations. Only recently has some aid been given to the living victims. But the damages to their lives will forever remain. The efforts by some national council of bishops tried to end the many practices and laws used to protect these predators. Even these changes can never be enough. I have argued that it is this universal long existing **clerical culture** that has brought about these **scandals** culminating in this horrific crisis. Unfortunately the crisis will not easily be resolved. It had been vividly captured by Geoffrey Chaucer in ***The Canterbury Tales*** many centuries ago. At the roots of this crisis exists the arrogance, the narcissism, the lust for wealth and power, as well as the sense of entitlement that is combined with the evolving deep sense of male superiority and self-righteous exclusivity. These elements of a ***world view*** are thoroughly embedded in this corrupt clerical culture. It is as if this ***world view*** is coded in the corrupt clerical cultures *very* DNA.

At the end of February 2019, Pope Francis and leaders of the councils of bishops from every nation gathered in the Vatican attempting to resolve this crisis. They tried to put an end to this violation of innocent human lives. But could they? Could they really confront this clerical culture in which they too are embedded? Could they enact the fundamental changes needed? Could they eradicate this practice of abuse and denial forever? Consider these questions. Could these leaders of the world's Catholic Communities speak more than platitudes of contrition and promises to act? Could they accept revolutionary changes to uproot this corrupt clerical culture? Could they take the revolutionary steps to punish all the perpetrators? Could they treat them as the criminals they truly are? Could they surrender them to the criminal courts for trial and punishment? Could they expose all those bishops who covered up these crimes, remove them from office and surrender them to punishment in criminal courts? The answer that emerged from this meeting was a resounding *No! We will not accept nor are we prepared to do anything so radical or so revolutionary at this time*. It seems clear that neither Pope Francis nor the council of bishops have heard the cry of the victims. *Non action speaks so loudly that we can't hear what you are saying*. However the Council of Bishops in the United States would have the victims and Catholics world–wide believe that they have devised a way to adequately address this crisis. It is a solution *made in the U.S.A* written all over it. **Throw lots of money at it.** Even this attempt has the *stench* of the **corrupt clerical culture.** Led by prominent leaders within the Council, many imbued with a fortune 500 C.E.O. attitude, they have amassed a vast sum estimated in billions of dollars. This fund is to be managed by professionals in the field of victim compensation. These gentle **men** have presided over the distribution of funds distributed to victims of many natural and man-made disasters. They are presented as the clerical culture's demonstration of charity and justice for all. But there is a catch. The claim is that these experts are totally independent of the clerical culture's influence and decision-making apparatus. This is not true. Their decisions must also be approved by the bishop council's leaders. So the leadership at the core of the corrupt clerical culture in America continues to absolve itself of any moral responsibilities. Now in play is the pretense allocating all decisions moral judgments and accountability to a group of *independent* and respected gentlemen. They are financial experts. They are a very experienced assemblage of laymen who have adjudicated disaster victims needs in many parts of the world. This purports to somehow address the Scandals in the

Catholic Church. It does not even come close. These insufficient actions, these claims of justice, fail miserably to address the damage of these horrific life violating crimes. The unmasking of theses incidences of past *Scandals in the Catholic Church is non ending* .Many had hoped that the new Pope Francis, the fourth pope following Pope John XXIII, would unlike his three predecessors, initiate the needed revolution to root out the **true causes** of these scandals.

All his efforts thus far have collapsed. The **world views** long embraced by many so called traditionalist Catholic leaders in positions of power are arrayed against him.

The utter failure of the February 2019 special council of bishops has doubtlessly forcefully demonstrated this. *Situation Normal...* It is evident that this clerical culture has been entrenched for many centuries is presently in control. It is alive within the present majority of Catholic leadership. It is this clerical culture that is in power with its deep-rooted privileges and its over-riding value of self-preservation.

(This is what has engendered, permitted and perpetuated these scandals.)

Catholics have always been taught to honor and respect all members of this clerical caste. I maintain that only a profound radical forward looking revolution greater than any ever envisioned by previous Ecumenical Councils can resolve these great *Scandals in the Catholic Church*. This would mean *eliminating entirely* this corrupt clerical culture with its hypocritical immoral world view. This is the corrupt culture that **devalues women, despises homosexuality, distorts human sexuality and denies the validity of other religious faiths. It ultimately denies the basic dignity and equality of every human being.** This radical revolution brought about by a future Ecumenical Council seems very unlikely and even impossible. Perhaps it is. At the end the 20th century John Lennon composed and sang this magnificent song: *Imagine.* In it are the words, ***Imagine all the people sharing all the world.*** We who have such an **imagination** are considered **idealists, impractical dreamers with no sense of reality**. At last greater numbers of us **dreamers** are beginning to understand that all the peoples of the world are more connected to one another than we ever thought. As the book of Genesis teaches:

All *of mankind is created by God in his own image.*

Our equality and dignity as human beings is founded upon this belief. A very wise Catholic moral theologian often taught his students- (I *among them*) ***If you are not willing to genuflect before each one of your fellow human beings then, do not bother to genuflect in the practice of your presumed faith.*** In our world of entrenched leadership behavior it seems nearly impossible to hold fast to our dreams of eliminating the corrupt clerical culture. Nevertheless many of us remain Catholic Christians. We must never forget what the great *Scandals in the Catholic Church* have finally and irrevocably unmasked. We look to a future when a great number of dedicated women and men of the entire Catholic Church community are inspired by a birth of revolutionary renewal in their *religious thought*. Then they can finally bring about what is truly needed. This is the sea change that is so desired by all thoughtful Catholic Christians. The prayer of the earliest Christians must be theirs as well.

Come Lord!

Epilogue

After all that has been written here there still remains the need for some further emphasis and clarification. This book has a dominant theme. It has advanced an uncommon difficult way of religious thinking. It presents a challenge to many long held practices. Many of these are founded upon ancient falsehoods, superstitions, ignorance, misinterpretations and political expediency. Our Platonic Aristotelian Western Greek reasoning structures that are our philosophically based logical inductive and deductive thinking processes are firmly embedded in our way of relating to the world. In existentialist terminology this foundational way of thinking *is our being toward the world*. In all science, art and literature this logical, analytical and creative thinking has served mankind **with notable exceptions** exceedingly well. But in **religious thinking** I maintain that we must adopt a different belief structure i.e. a different religious **world view**. The very survival of mankind may depend on it. This different religious belief structure proposed here adheres more closely to the paradoxes of Asian and African religious thinking. This may be best expressed by this principle. *In religious thought:* there ought to be *no absolutes, no One way,* **no** *One understanding,* **no** *One way* **of seeing the world and our place in it.** This means there are *many ways* we as human beings can interpret our experiences; different ways we can shape and value the world and express that value. Throughout our history we have taken different attitudes toward death, life, sexuality and power. Many people who are thoughtful in their different traditions are very much concerned with how we can live in such a *pluralistic world*. How do Christians in particular deal with other religious faiths they have always believed inferior to their own? Can Christians, Jews, Muslims and all the other great religious traditions acknowledge the *validity* of each other's and other great religious traditions? There seems to be no historical evidence for affirming this choice among nearly all these many traditions.

But in our century we are forced to hold fast to *a pluralistic world*, a world without religious absolutes. We must *imagine* such a world becoming a reality in the future.

I maintain that this position is central, even essential, to the message of this book.

The great Nigerian novelist/philosopher, Chinua Achebe in his 1960's Interviews with Bill Moyers presented this paradox when explaining an ancient Nigerian proverb: Whenever one finds a truth there is always another standing next to it; even sometimes in opposition to it. St. Thomas Aquinas, the paragon of Catholic theology approached this position. Late in his life he discovered that his renowned *proof* for the existence of one God could also be employed with little difficulty to prove the existence of many Gods or at least many aspects of a single God. I advocate that this principle- **pluralistic validity should be held by all religious people.** It is while they firmly accept the faith they have hopefully *freely chosen* to believe and live, it is necessary that they accept the reality that there are meaningful beliefs, different faiths that may be as valid as their own. Therefore, an authentic Catholic may firmly believe the mystery of a Trinitarian God, i.e. Father, Son and Holy Spirit. Nevertheless authentic Catholic faith must respect and honor other beliefs that may completely contradict its own. The Catholic must accept that faith is a choice. **This is its strength. It is not its weakness.** A Catholic ought to be living the proposition:

Love *Thy Neighbor As Thyself*.

Epilogue

Religious fanaticism maintains there is only **One Way, One Truth, One valid belief**. That there is only one acceptable religious belief is truly **fanaticism**. It is Elie Wiesel who wrote,

"Fanaticism is the greatest danger to mankind."

But **fanaticism** is the force so dominant in religious thought and practice. History consistently proclaims that **fanaticism** in any form whether it is Christianity, Islam, Judaism, Hinduism, Buddhism, Tribalism and yes, even Atheism, **always** produces the ultimate tragedy for humanity. The long-standing practice of **fanaticism** produced atrocities that were always justified by the mantra of the papal inspired Crusades

"God Will it!

It produced the madness of the violence of Rome, the wars of early and continuous Christianity and the murders of the Inquisition. It produced the religious horrors of the Crusades, the slaughter of Jews by Christians and Christians by Christians. **Fanaticism** has produced the millions executed by Nazi white supremacists in the genocide attempts of the Holocaust. It has also produced genocides continuing in our time. Today, to the shock of Catholics world-wide, **fanaticism** has produced the ongoing great scandals of sexual violation of innocent children by many clergymen. These corrupt shepherds often spoke the very words *God wills it* as they violated their victims. Compounding this horror is the continual, criminal attempts to deny while covering it up. All this was proclaimed to be in order to ***protect the Catholic People***. In reality it has never been to protect the people of Christian faith, the clean sheep.

> *(So the cover-up always was to safeguard the wealth and reputations of the Catholic leadership and all lesser ranks of the*

clergy caste. It was to hide the horrible behavior of the astonishingly large numbers of Catholic clergy of all ranks)

𝕷𝖊𝖘𝖘 𝖙𝖍𝖊 𝖕𝖔𝖔𝖗 𝖘𝖍𝖊𝖊𝖕 𝖙𝖔 𝖑𝖔𝖘𝖊 𝖙𝖗𝖚𝖘𝖙𝖊.

Among these poor sheep are the many innocent victims who may have lost trust but are valued by all Catholic people of faith. They will always remain the clean sheep who are loved by **The Good Shepherd present in the midst of His flock***.* This is what St. Augustine, the Bishop of Hippo meant proclaiming to the Christian people there while distributing the Eucharist to each one: **You are the Body of Christ!**

At the end of the decade of change, the 1960's, arrived my last meeting with the Bishop of Adamsburgh who had supported me for many years. He had honored me to explain the proposals of Vatican II as best I could. *(But I never did influence most of his priests.)* So in Synagogues, Christian Churches, in both religious and secular Colleges and as a lector in Catholic Colleges I was his spokesperson on ***the changes in the entire Catholic_Church Community***. This was also on Radio, Television and in the Press. With disappointment and great reluctance his office after his death granted me permission to seek papal dispensation to end obligations of celibacy. But it was only on condition that I would never act as a Catholic priest except at the request of a Catholic near death. This dispensation called a ***re-script,*** as noted before, was as complicated in its application and as long in its coming. Continuing my graduate education, I taught in college, married, raised two children, and worked in the corporate world as a research consultant. I was even elected mayor of a small city. I have continually tried to live a life following the prescription of a 7th century Hindu poet and philosopher:

All the *happiness* in the world is brought about by those who seek the happiness of others. While all the *misery* in the world is brought by those who seek only their own happiness.

Epilogue

(As I approach my 90th year, this is still a work-in-progress.)

It's clear that an elimination of the clerical culture must be replaced by radical restructuring the leadership in the entire Catholic Church. Though not needing the elimination of the priesthood leadership itself, it will definitely require bold structural changes unheard of since the earliest days of Christianity's formation. It will certainly involve leadership roles for ***both*** genders. It will include both married and celibate, a truly **pluralistic society** different from the present one. It must engage in its leadership **all persons** of clearly demonstrated wisdom, authenticity, integrity and maturity. It may even have a democratic term limited election processes.

***What it must have is* a method of continuous self- evaluation/review, as well as a term limited and respected elected** *Supreme Judicial Component.* This **society** must also have the authority to remove any of the corrupt attitudes beliefs and practices of the many past centuries.

If this book *accomplishes anything* it will have awakened **the existential need to eliminate this century's old, immoral, authoritarian and corrupt clerical culture in the entire Catholic Christian Community.**

Never must the *Leaven of the Pharisees* spread like cancer among the shepherds of **The Mystical Body of Christ**-the Community of Christian People, the "sheep" so beloved by the *Good Shepherd*. This cancer finally now becoming fully unmasked, after centuries of abominable crimes and despicable corruption this clerical culture is truly the ultimate:

SCANDAL IN THE CATHOLIC CHURCH.

This radical restructuring of this revolution is the monumental task that this book proclaims is ***essential*** for the survival of the Catholic Church in the 21ˢᵗ century. As a Catholic Christian, nearly 90 years of age, I will not see this needed revolution. Nor is it likely to come soon. However, I continue to believe **it will come**. We can **imagine** it. We can even see *indications* of its coming.

Because of the intense bombing of European cities during World War II many church buildings were either destroyed or severely damaged. This included some of the great cathedrals. As reconstruction began it was discovered that the most sacred sections of these churches, the sanctuaries, could not be restored immediately. Architects and construction workers found that the sanctuaries of the cathedrals and most early Christian churches had been built on top of the temples of ancient religions such as Druid and unnamed "pagan" cults. Recent scholarship has also found that many of these "pagan:" customs, holidays, rites and festivals had been modified and converted or absorbed into early Christian holidays and festivals. So not only did the early Christian communities absorb the "pagan" temples by building over them but they absorbed the valuable elements of the cultures whose **world views** and practices they were replacing. They were actually "baptizing" them into Christianity.

We **dreamers** dare to imagine that in the future, perhaps later in the 21ˢᵗ century a new generation of young thoughtful people of faith will be unafraid to create a renewed **one world faithful community**. Perhaps they will have overcome the present tide of more absolutist **fanatical self-described traditionalists Catholics** who have been seizing positions of power in legislatures, judicial offices, educational organizations, and corporate structures in many nations including our own. It is taking place in the early part of this current century. This group of **self-righteous religious fanatics** has been amassing vast sums of money to advance their **distorted supremacist authoritarian world**

view. They truly believe that thirty pieces of silver will guarantee their success. I do not believe it will. **All human history proclaims that absolutist fanatics have always failed!**

Will this hoped for new generation of thoughtful renewed Christians, to whom a new torch has yet to be passed, act as those early Christians did? Will they also learn to embrace and build upon the vales of the continually rapidly being discovered political structures, visual art forms, literature, music, and yes, the amazing scientific discoveries? Will they create that new birth of freedom in **a renewed pluralistic society**? Will they learn to **sing a brand new song to the Lord and bless His Name**?

There is **hope** for the future **always**. In the final words of the New Testament once again:

MARAN ATHA- COME LORD

Appendix J

Authors whose words are cited in the text

CHAUCER, GEOFREY, Harrison. Marilee, **English History Publisher,** November 18, 2021

MERTON, Thomas. *Conjectures of a Guilty Bystander,* **Doubleday Pub.***1955*

PECK, M. Scott, T*he Road Less Traveled,* **Simon & Shuster** 1978

DICKENS, Charles. *A Tale of Two Cities* **Signet Reissue Editions**, 2007

WIESEL, Elie, *NIGHT,* ***Premium Books***, 2006

Appendix JJ

A SELECT BIBLIOGRAPHY OF AUTHORS AND THEIR WORKS THAT HAVE INSPIRED THE THOUGHTS OF THIS WRITER FOR MANT YEARS

CONGAR, Yves M.J., *Lay People in the Church*. **Geoffrey Chapman.1959**

SINGER, Peter, *One World*, **Yale University Press. 2002**

DONDAYNE, Albert, *Contemporary Thought and Christian Faith* .**Duquesne University Press, 1958**

BAUM, Gregory, *Journal of Ecumenical Studies*. **Cross Currents Publishers Inc.,, 1981**

SCHILLEBEECKX, Edward *JESUS, an Experiment in Christology,* **Crossroad Publishing Company, 1981**

RIDEAU, Emile, *The Thought of Teilhard de Chardin*, **Harper & Row. 1967**

RYNNE, Xavier, *Letters From Vatican City*, **Farrar, Straus & Co.1963**

SMITH, Huston, *World's Religions*, **Harper Collins Publishers**, **1995**

CORWELL, John. *Hitler's Pope*, **Penguin Putnam Inc., 1999**

WILLS, Gary, *Papal Sin,* **Random House Inc., 2000**

PIEPER, Josef, The Negative Element in the Philosophy of Thomas Aquinas. **Cross Currents Publishers Inc., 1953**

MOYERS, Bill, *A World of Ideas,* **Doubleday Dell Publishers, 1989**

BRONOWSKI, Jacob, *A SENSE OF THE FUTURE,* **The MIT Press, 1977**

TUCHMAN, Barbara W, *The March of Folly,* **Alfred A. Knoff, 1984**

BERGSON, Henri, *The Two Sources of Morality and Religion,*(English translation)

University of Notre Dame Press, 1977

Acknowledgement: The thoughts of these authors have greatly inspired the evolution of my thinking in the more than fifty years this book has been thoughtfully in development.

My debt of gratitude to them is beyond measure.